GENERAL

on

INDIA

By
T.S. Kuppusamy, B.A., D.L.S.

EDITION
2002

SURA COLLEGE OF COMPETITION
Chennai ● Bangalore ● Kolkata

Price: Rs.18.00

© PUBLISHERS

General Knowledge on INDIA

Price: Rs.18.00
ISBN: 81-7254-145-7

Sura College of Competition,

- 1620, 'J' Block,
  16th Main Road,
  Anna Nagar,
  Chennai - 600 040.
  Phones: 91-44-6266173, 6266524

Printed at **T. Krishna Press,** Chennai - 600 102 and Published
by **V.V.K.Subbaraj** for **Sura College of Competition,**
1620, 'J' Block, 16th Main Road, Anna Nagar, Chennai -
600040. Phone: 91-44-6266173, 6266524. Fax: (91) 44-
6266173. email: surabooks@eth.net

CONTENTS

GENERAL KNOWLEDGE
ON
INDIA

Part-I ⬇ **1. HISTORICAL EVENTS**

S.No.	Year	Events
1.	1857	Sepoy revolt against the military officers in Meerut.
2.	1857-1858	Sepoys march to Delhi - revolts spread to other parts of India - revolt crushed
3.	2.8.1858	Power transferred from East India Company to British Crown.
4.	1885	Indian National Congress founded. - W.C. Banerjee 1st president.
5.	1893	Mohandas Karamchand Gandhi landed in Durban, South Africa.
6.	1904-1906	Dhadabai Naoroji, Gopalakrishna Gokhale & Bala Gangadhar Tilak demanded Self Government.
7.	1911	Viceregal Headquarters transferred from Calcutta to Delhi.
8.	1915	Mohandas Karamchand Gandhi returned to India.
9.	1916	Tilak, Annie Besant started Home Rule movement.
10.	1919	Britain passed Government of India Act to pave way for Indians to play major role in running its own Government. But Viceroys and Governors were given overriding power. Indians dissatisfied.
11.	1919	Mahatma Gandhi began a campaign of Passive Resistance to British rule in India. Protest against Rowlatt Act.

S.No.	Year	Events
12.	13.4.1919	Jalianwalla Bagh massacre by General Dyre, in Amritsar killing 379 Indians. 1200 were wounded.
13.	1920-1921	Indian National Congress under Mahatma Gandh; boycotted foreign cloth and picketted toddy shops.
14.	1929	Poorna Swaraj demanded by Indian National Congress.
15.	1930	Salt Satyagraha, Dandi March by Mahatma Gandhi, Vedaranyam March by Rajaji in Madras Presidency.
16.	1935	Government of India Act passed to pave way for federal system in Indian Government
17.	1938-1939	Independence struggle in Princely States.
18.	9.8.1942	**Quit India** movement with slogan **Do or Die** by Mahatma Gandhi.
19.	1946	Interim Government formed with Jawaharlal Nehru as Prime Minister.
20.	9.12.1946	Constituent Assembly was formed to frame Constitution for Independent India.
21.	20.2.1947	British Government announced withdrawal from India.
22.	14.8.1947	Pakistan founded bifurcating India.
23.	15.8.1947	India became independent with Jawaharlal Nehru as Prime Minister.
24.	26.11.1949	Indian Constitution adopted declaring India Sovereign Socialist Secular Democratic Republic.
25.	26.01.1950	India became Republic.

2. BRITISH MONARCHS (Emperors)

1.	**Queen Victoria** (1837-1901)	Ruled India 1858-1901
2.	**Edward VII** (1901 - 1910)	1901-1910
3.	**George V** (1910-1936)	1910-1936
4.	**Edward VIII** (1936 abdicated)	1936

5.	George VI (1936-1952), King	1936-1947, 1947-1950

3. BRITISH PROVINCES

S.No.	Name	HQ
1.	Assam	Shillong
2.	Baluchistan	Quetta
3.	Bengal Presidency	Calcutta
4.	Bihar (Bifurcated from Bengal 1912)	Patna
5.	Bombay Presidency	Bombay
6.	Central Province	Nagpur
7.	Delhi (From 1912)	New Delhi
8.	Madras Presidency	Madras
9.	North West Frontier (1932 - became province)	Peshawar
10.	Orissa (Bifurcated from Bihar in 1935)	Cuttack
11.	Punjab	Lahore
12.	Sind	Hyderabad
13.	United Provinces	Lucknow

BRITISH PROVINCES - 1947

(Bifurcated from India)

S.No.	Name	HQ
	PAKISTAN - 1947	KARACHI
1.	Baluchistan	Quetta
2.	N.W. Frontier	Peshawar
3.	Punjab (West)	Lahore
4.	Sind	Hyderabad
5.	Bengal (East)	Dhaka
6.	14 Princely States acceded to Pakistan.	
	Total Area.	8,03,943 Sq km.

BANGLADESH-1971	DHAKA
1. East Bengal after liberation from Pakistan	Dhaka
Total Area	1,44,020 Sq.km

4. INDIAN PROVINCES - 1947
(After bifurcation)

S.No.	'A' States	HQ
1.	Assam	Shillong
2.	Bengal (West)	Calcutta
3.	Bihar	Patna
4.	Bombay	Bombay
5.	Central Province	Nagpur
6.	Madras	Madras
7.	Orissa	Cuttack
8.	Punjab (East)	Chandigarh
9.	United Province (Uttar Pradesh)	Lucknow

'B' States and territories

562 Princely States amalgamated into Indian Union	Formed as 26 of 'B' States and territories

5. NEIGHBOURING COUNTRIES

1.	**North**	China, Nepal, Bhutan
2.	**Northwest**	Afghanistan
3.	**West**	Pakistan
4.	**East**	Bangladesh
5.	**South**	Sri Lanka.

On 15th August 1947

Long years ago we made a tryst with destiny and now the time comes when we shall redeem our pledge, not wholly or in full measure, but very substantially. At the stroke of midnight hour, when the world sleeps, India will awake to life and freedom.

- Jawaharlal Nehru.

6. INDEPENDENT INDIA
(Dominion Status)
15.8.1947 to 25.1.1950

1.	Governor-General (Appointed by King of United Kingdom)	**1. Lord Mountbatten.** (15.8.1947 to 20.6.1948) **2. C. Rajagopalachari** (21.6.1948 to 25.1.1950)
2.	Prime Minister	**Jawaharlal Nehru**
3.	Speaker, Parliament	**G.V. Mavlankar**
4.	Chief Justice, Federal Court	**Justice H.R. Kania**

7. FIRST INDIAN CABINET
(15.8.1947)

S.No.	Name of the Minister	Portfolio
1.	Jawaharlal Nehru	Prime Minister, External Affairs and Commonwealth Affairs.
2.	Sardar Vallabhai Patel	Deputy Prime Minister, Home, States and Information and Broadcasting
3.	Dr. Rajendra Prasad	Food and Agriculture
4.	Maulana Abul Kalaam Azad	Education
5.	John Mathai	Railways and Transport
6.	Jagjivan Ram	Labour
7.	C.H. Babha	Commerce
8.	Rafi Ahmed Kidwai	Communications
9.	Sardar Baldev Singh	Defence
10.	Rajkumari Amrit Kaur	Health
11.	Dr. B.R. Ambedkhar	Law
12.	R.K. Shanmugam Chetty	Finance
13.	S.P. Mukerjee	Industry and Supply
14.	N.V. Gadgil	Works, Mines, Power.

8. INDIAN CONSTITUTION
(Drafting Committee)
(Constituted on 28.8.1947)

1.	**Chairman**	Dr. B.R. Ambedkhar
2.	**Members**	1. N.Gopalasamy Ayyangar
		2. Allady Krishnasamy Ayyar
		3. K.M. Munshi
		4. Md. Sadulla
		5. B.L. Mitter (Resigned)
		Madhava Rao
		6. Dr. K.P. Kaitan (Died)
		T.T. Krishnamachari
3.	**Constitutional Advisor**	B. Narasinga Rao

9. THE CONSTITUTION OF INDIAN REPUBLIC

We, THE PEOPLE OF INDIA, having solemnly resolved to constitute India into a **SOVEREIGN SOCIALIST SECULAR DEMOCRATIC REPUBLIC** and to secure to all its citizens,

JUSTICE, social, economic and political

LIBERTY of thought, expression, belief, faith and worship.

EQUALITY of status and of opportunity; and to promote among them all

FRATERNITY, assuring the dignity of the individual and the unity of the nation.

IN OUR CONSTITUENT ASSEMBLY, this twentysixth day of November 1949, do HEREBY ADOPT, ENACT AND GIVE TO OURSELVES THIS **CONSTITUTION**.

10. INDIAN CONSTITUTION
(Important Features)

1.	**Political Characteristics**	Sovereign Socialist Secular Democratic Republic

2.	**Form of Government**	Parliamentary form, based on adult franchise
3.	**Distinct Features**	1. Fundamental Rights enforceable by courts
		2. Directive Principles of State policy for people's welfare
4.	**Constitution adopted on**	26.11.1949
5.	**Constitution came into force**	26.01.1950

11. FUNDAMENTAL RIGHTS

1.	**Right to Equality**	1. Equality before Law
		2. Social equality
		3. Equality of opportunity in public appointment
2.	**Right to Freedom**	Freedom of Speech and Expression, Assembly, Association, Movement, Residence, acquisition and disposition of property. Right to practise any profession or to carry on any occupation, trade or business.
		Right to property is no more Fundamental Rights.
3.	**Right against exploitation**	Right forbids, slave traffic in human beings, beggary, in any form of forced labour
	a) State can enforce	Compulsory military training and military and industrial conscript
4.	**Right to Freedom of Religion**	Freedom of religion

allow everyone to entertain any notion to exhibit his sentiments in such form of worship, but not injurious to the equal rights of others, all subject to public order, morality and health.

5. **Cultural and Educational Rights** — Any section of citizen having a distinct language script or culture of its own have the right to conserve the same

12. SCHEDULES OF CONSTITUTION

1. **First Schedule** — List of States and Territories
2. **Second Schedule** — Remuneration and emoluments to Constitutional Authorities
3. **Third Schedule** — Forms of Oaths and Affirmations
4. **Fourth Schedule** — Allocation of Seats in Rajya Sabha
5. **Fifth Schedule** — Administration of Scheduled areas
6. **Sixth Schedule** — Administration of Tribal areas
7. **Seventh Schedule** — List of Subjects, Central, States and Concurrent.
8. **Eighth Schedule** — List of National Languages
9. **Ninth Schedule** — Acts and orders relating to land tenures
10. **Tenth Schedule** — Anti-defection Act
11. **Eleventh Schedule** — Panchayat Raj system
12. **Twelfth Schedule** — 3 types of Municipalities

13. IMPORTANT CONSTITUTIONAL AMENDMENTS

1. **7th Amendment Act, 1956** — After reorganisation of States, part A, B, C, States were abolished – Maximum Strength of Lok Sabha fixed at 525

2. **14th Amendment Act, 1962** — Confer legislative powers on Parliament to enact laws for creation of Legislature and Council of Ministers in Union Territories

3. **19th Amendment Act, 1966** — Art. 324 amended abolishing Election Tribunals, election petition to be heard by High Courts

4. **25th Amendment Act, 1971** — Property rights do not stand in the implementation of Directive Principles of State Policy

5. **31st Amendment Act, 1973** — Increased the upper limit of elective seats in the Lok Sabha from 525 to 545

6. **52nd Amendment Act, 1985** — The Bill was called Anti-Defection Bill, to curb defection by disqualification

7. **61st Amendment Act, 1989** — It lowers the voting age from 21 to 18

8. **74th Amendment Act, 1993 New part XI - A** — Constitution of 3 types of Municipalities, i.e., Nagar Panchayats, Municipal Councils and Municipal Corporations

9. **76th Amendment Act, 1994** — Tamil Nadu Reservation Bill within the purview of Ninth Schedule. 18% S.C. 1% S.T 50% B.C. (total 69%)

10. **Amendment Bill, 1996**	Ensures 33% reservation for women in Parliament and State Legislatures (pending in the Parliament)
11. **79th Amendment Act, 1999**	Reservation of S.C.s and S.T.s and Anglo Indians in Lok Sabha and State Assemblies extended for a further period of 10 years beyond January 25, 2000.
12. **80th Amendment Act, 2000**	It provides 29% of the total income obtained from central taxes and duties for distribution among the states with effect from 1.4.1996

14. NATIONAL SYMBOLS

NATIONAL FLAG

- ◆ Horizontal tricolour
- ◆ Deep Kesar (Saffron) on top
- ◆ White in middle,
- ◆ Dark Green at bottom in equal portion.
- ◆ In the centre of the white band
  Wheel in Navy Blue with 24 spokes.
  (Adopted by Constituent Assembly on 22.1.1947)

NATIONAL ANTHEM

"**Jana Gana Mana** ....." composed by Rabindranath Tagore adopted as National Anthem of India on 24th January 1950.

The song was published in January 1912 under the title "Bhartat Vidhata" in the "Tatva Bodhini" patrika edited by Tagore. The same song was translated into English by Tagore in 1919 under the title "Morning Song of India".

NATIONAL SONG

"**Vande Mataram**" composed by Bankhim Chandra Chatterjee in his novel "**Anand Math**" published in 1882.

The song was a source of inspiration to the freedom fighters. It was sung in 1896 session of the Indian National Congress.

NATIONAL EMBLEM

The National Emblem and seal of the Government is a replica of the capitol (top part) of Asoka's pillar at Saranath.

There are four lions standing back to back with their mouths wide open, at the top. (Only three lions are visible)

At the bottom there is a "Dharmachakra" in the centre with figures of bull on the right and horse on the left.

The words "Sathyameva Jayate" inscribed below in Devanagari Script.

The word is taken from "Mundaka Upanishad". It means, "Truth Alone triumphs".

(This National Emblem was adopted on 26th January 1950 by the Government of India.)

NATIONAL CALENDER

Based on Saka Era (78.A.D.) with Chaitra as its first month falls on March 22 in a common year and 21st March in a leap year. Phalguna is the last month.

This Calendar was introduced in the year 1957 from March 22. (The day on which Kanishka, ascended the throne.)

NATIONAL ANIMAL

The majestic tiger - the Indian race is the Royal Bengal Tiger, seen throughout India. The animal is known for its illusive design and formidable power.

NATIONAL BIRD

The Indian peacock is the National Bird of India. The peacock has found its place in Indian Literature, folklore and legends. The bird is found throughout India.

NATIONAL FLOWER

Lotus is the National Flower. It has found its place in Indian Literature, folklore and legends.

NATIONAL TREE

Banyan Tree

15. NATIONAL LANGUAGES

S.No.	Language	State / States
1.	Assamese	Assam
2.	Bengali	West Bengal
3.	Gujarathi	Gujarat, Daman & Diu
4.	Hindi	Bihar, Haryana, Himachal Pradesh, Madhya Pradesh, Chandigarh, Rajasthan, Uttar Pradesh, Delhi
5.	Kannada	Karnataka
6.	Kashmiri	Jammu & Kashmir
7.	Konkani	Goa
8.	Malayalam	Kerala, Lakshadweep
9.	Manipuri	Manipur, Tripura
10.	Marathi	Maharashtra
11.	Nepali	Sikkim
12.	Oriya	Orissa
13.	Punjabi	Punjab, Chandigarh
14.	Sanskrit	Widely Spoken
15.	Sindhi	Widely Spoken
16.	Tamil	Tamil Nadu, Pondicherry
17.	Telugu	Andhra Pradesh
18.	Urdu	Andhra Pradesh, Kashmir, Uttar Pradesh

16. OFFICIAL LANGUAGE

Official Language (Article 343)

Official Language of the Union - Hindi in Devanagari Script.

English was continued to be used for all the official purposes - till 1965.

Official Languages Act, 1967

English shall be used for communication between the Union and the States which do not have Hindi as official language.

(English is the official language of 58 countries in the World)

17. PRINCIPAL RELIGIONS IN INDIA

(As per Census 1991)

1.	Hinduism	–	82.00%
2.	Islam	–	12.12%
3.	Christianity	–	2.34%
4.	Sikhism	–	1.94%
5.	Buddhism	–	0.76%
6.	Jainism	–	0.39%
7.	Others	–	0.05%

18. NATIONAL HOLIDAYS AND INDIAN STANDARD TIME

1. National Holidays

1. Republic Day (26th January)
2. Independence Day (15th August)
3. Gandhi Jayanthi (2nd October)

2. Indian Standard Time

It is fixed on the mean time of $82\frac{1}{2}°$ (E) meridian which passes through near Allahabad.

(5 Hrs and 30 Mts of Greenwich Time ahead)

Greenwich Mean Time

It is based on the local time of the meridian passing through Greenwich near London. (It is standard time of U.K.)

Local Time for any place

It varies from the Greenwich time at the rate of 4 minutes for each degree of Longitude.

19. INDIAN CURRENCY

One Rupee = 16 Annas
One Anna   = 12 Paise

In 1957 Decimal System was introduced.

One Rupee = 100 Paise

Weights and Measures

Metric System was introduced in October 1958.

Length	:	Foot, Yard, Furlong, Mile (converted to)
		Centimetre, Meter, Kilometre.
Mass	:	Ounce, Pound, Stone, Ton (converted to)
		Gram, Kilogram, Tonne.
Volume	:	Fluid Ounce, Pint, Gallon (converted to)
		Millilitre, Litre.

20. IMPORTANT DAYS IN THE YEAR

1.	Sarvodaya Day	**31st January**
2.	Teachers Day	**5th September**
3.	National Solidarity Day	**31st October**
4.	Children's Day	**14th November**
5.	National Integration Day	**19th November**

21. INDIA - PHYSICAL FEATURES

1.	**Headquarters**	New Delhi
2.	**Area**	32,87,263 Sq. Km.
	North to South	3214 Kms.
	East to West	2933 Kms.
3.	**Population (2001)**	102.7 Crores
	Literacy (2001)	Males: 75.85%, Females: 54.15%
4.	**Physical Characteristics**	1. Great Mountain Zone
		2. Indo-Gangetic plain
		3. Desert Region
		4. Southern Peninsula
5.	**Major Rivers**	1. Ganga 2. Yamuna
		3. Indus 4. Beas
		5. Sutlej
		6. Brahmaputra
		7. Godavari 8. Krishna
		9. Narmada 10. Tapti
		11. Mahanadi 12. Pennar
		13. Cauveri 14. Palar
		15. Vaigai
		16. Thamarabharani

6. **No. of States in the Union**
   a) No.of States   28
   b) No.of Territories   7
7. **No. of Ports (Major)**   12
8. **Metropolitan cities**   Mumbai (12.6 Millions)
                               Kolkata (11.02 Millions)
                               Delhi (8.42 Millions)
                               Chennai (5.42 Millions)
9. **Other largest cities**   1. Ahmedabad, 2. Bangalore
                               3. Hyderabad   4. Jaipur
                               5. Kanpur   6. Lucknow
                               7. Nagpur   8. Pune
                               9. Allahabad

22. STATES REORGANISATION

1. **1947**   British ruled provinces, were called 'A' States.

                   Princely States were called 'B' States.

                   Other territories were called 'C' States.

2. **1953**   Andhra State was formed bifurcating Madras Presidency.

3. **1956**   States were re-organised on linguistic basis. (1) A & B States were merged and demarcated and brought under two groups, called (a) States (b) Territories.

                   (2) Madhya Pradesh formed merging Madhya Bharat, Mahakoshal, Bhopal and Vindhya Pradesh.

4. **1956**   Andhra Pradesh was formed merging Hyderabad State with Andhra State.

5. **1959**   Gujarat was formed bifurcating Bombay Presidency.

6.	**1961 Dec., 20**	Goa, Diu, Daman were liberated from Portuguese became Indian territory
7.	**1963**	Pondicherry merged with India became Indian territory.
8.	**1963**	Nagaland attained Statehood.
9.	**1966**	Haryana State formed bifurcating Punjab and Chandigarh became territory.
10.	**1971**	Himachal Pradesh attained Statehood.
11.	**1972**	Assam State re-organised carving out Meghalaya, Manipur, Tripura as States. Arunachal Pradesh and Mizoram as territories
12.	**1975 May 16**	Sikkim (Himalayan State) merged with Indian Union as 22nd State.
13.	**1986**	Mizoram and Arunachal Pradesh attained Statehood.
14.	**1987**	Goa attained Statehood. Daman, Diu continue, to be territories
15.	**1994**	Delhi attained Statehood.
16.	**2000, Nov. 1**	Chattisgarh formed bifurcating 16 districts of Madhya Pradesh.
17.	**2000, Nov. 9**	Uttaranchal formed bifurcating 13 hill districts of Uttar Pradesh.
18.	**2000, Nov. 15**	Jharkhand formed bifurcating 18 districts of Bihar.

RAJASTHAN STATE

Amalgamation of Princely States

1. Ajmer	2. Alwar	3. Banswara
4. Barmer	5. Bharatpur	6. Bhilwara
7. Bikaner	8. Bundhi	9. Chittorgarh
10. Churu	11. Dholpur	12. Dungarpur
13. Ganga Nagar	14. Jalore	15. Jaipur
16. Jaisalmer	17. Jhalawar	18. Jhunjhunu

19. Jhodhpur	20. Kota	21. Nagaur
22. Pali	23. Sawai Madhopur	24. Sikar
25. Sirohi	26. Tonk	27. Udaipur

23. CAPITAL CITY - NEW DELHI

1. Indian Union
   Headquarters   **New Delhi**
   Established in 1911 southern
   part of Delhi
   a) Ancient Name   **Indraprastha**
   b) Shah Jahan in 1638 named it   **Delhi**
   c) Red Fort built.   **1648**

2. Metropolitan Area   **1483 Sq. Km.**
   Population   **137.8 lakhs.**
   Literacy   **81.8%**
   Density (per sq. km.)   **9,294**

1. **Delhi (City State)**   **Constituted in 1970**
2. Revenue units   **4**
3. Constituencies
   a) Parliament   **7**
   b) Assembly   **70**

National Headquarters

1. Places comprising   Rashtrapathi Bhavan
                                                  Parliament House
                                                  Supreme Court

23-A. RASHTRAPATHI BHAVAN

1. Originally it was vice-regal residence
2. Completed and occupied by Viceroy in the year 1929
3. Architects: Edwin Luteyens and Herbert Baker
4. Cost   14 Million Rupees
5. Rooms   340
   a) Consists of   **(1)** Durbar Hall   **(2)** Council Hall
                             (3) Ashoka Hall   **(4)** Library
                             (5) Printing Press   **(6)** Art Gallery
                             (7) Theatre   **(8)** Hall of gifts.

24. STATES

S. No.	Name of the State	Population	Literacy rate	Area Sq.Km	Voters lakhs (1991)	L.S seats	R.S seats	Head- Quarters
1.	Andhra Pradesh	7,57,27,541	61.1%	276.0	476.32	42	18	Hyderabad
2.	Arunachal Pradesh	10,91,117	54.7%	83.7	5.32	2	1	Ita Nagar
3.	Assam	2,66,38,407	64.3%	79.0	122.69	14	7	Dispur
4.	Bihar	8,28,78,796	47.5%	94.16	-	40	16	Patna
5.	Chhattisgarh	2,07,75,956	65.2%	135.1	-	11	16	Raipur
6.	Goa	13,43,998	82.3%	4.0	8.22	2	1	Panaji
7.	Gujarat	5,05,96,992	70.0%	196.0	290.22	26	11	Gandhi Nagar
8.	Haryana	2,10,82,989	68.6%	44.2	113.16	10	5	Chandigarh
9.	Himachal Pradesh	60,77,248	77.1%	56.0	33.2	4	3	Simla
10.	Jammu & Kashmir	1,00,69,917	54.5%	222.0	42.71	6	4	Jammu & Srinagar
11.	Jharkhand	2,69,09,428	54.1%	79.71	-	14	6	Ranchi
12.	Karnataka	5,27,33,958	67.0%	191.7	316.26	28	12	Bangalore
13.	Kerala	3,18,36,619	90.9%	39.0	203.79	20	9	Thiruvanan-thapuram
14.	Madhya Pradesh	6,03,85,118	64.1%	307.9	-	29	11	Bhopal
15.	Maharashtra	9,67,52,247	77.3%	308.0	350.74	48	19	Mumbai
16.	Manipur	23,88,634	68.9%	22.3	12.67	2	1	Imphal
17.	Meghalaya	23,06,069	63.3%	22.4	10.86	2	1	Shillong
18.	Mizoram	8,91,058	88.5%	21.0	3.95	1	1	Aizawl
19.	Nagaland	19,88,636	67.1%	17.0	8.47	1	1	Kohima
20.	Orissa	3,67,06,920	63.6%	156.0	270.68	21	10	Bhubaneshwar
21.	Punjab	2,42,89,296	70.0%	50.3	148.00	13	7	Chandigarh
22.	Rajasthan	5,64,73,122	61.0%	342.2	299.13	25	10	Jaipur
23.	Sikkim	5,40,493	69.7%	7.0	2.17	1	1	Gangtok
24.	Tamil Nadu	6,21,10,839	73.5%	130.0	420.97	39	18	Chennai
25.	Tripura	31,91,168	73.7%	10.4	15.78	2	1	Agartala
26.	Uttar Pradesh	16,60,52,859	57.4%	238.55	-	80	31	Lucknow
27.	Uttaranchal	84,79,562	72.3%	55.85	-	5	3	Dehradun
28.	West Bengal	8,02,21,171	69.2%	88.7	446.73	42	16	Kolkata

Union territories

S. No.	Name	Population	Literacy rate	Area Sq.Km	Voters lakhs (1991)	L.S seats	R.S seats	Head- Quarters
1.	Delhi	1,37,82,976	81.8%	1.5	84.98	7	4	New Delhi
2.	Andaman & Nicobar Islands	3,56,265	81.2%	8.24	1.61	1	1	Port Blair
3.	Chandigarh	9,00,914	81.8%	0.114	3.77	1	1	Chandigarh
4.	Dadra & Nagar Haveli	2,20,451	60.0%	0.5	0.57	1	1	Silvassa
5.	Daman & Diu	1,58,059	81.1%	0.112	0.74	1	1	Daman
6.	Lakshadweep	60,595	87.5%	0.03	0.30	1	-	Kavaratti
7.	Pondicherry	9,73,829	81.5%	0.5	5.91	1	1	Pondicherry

25. PRESIDENT OF INDIA

1.	**Head of the Republic**	The President of India
2.	**Elected by**	Electoral college
	a) Electoral College	Elected members of Lok Sabha, Rajya Sabha and Legislatures in the Union.
3.	**Term**	5 years
4.	**Residence**	Rashtrapathi Bhavan
5.	**Powers and Duties**	1. Supreme Commander of Defence Forces
		2. All executive functions of Union Govt.
		3. To give assent to law
		4. To address Parliament joint session at the commencement of session every year.
6.	**Monthly Salary**	Rs.10,000/- raised to Rs. 20,000/- From 1.1.96 revised at Rs. 50,000/- per month
	a) **Pension**	Rs. 3 lakhs per annum

Presidents of India

1.	Dr. Rajendra Prasad	1950 - 52
		1952 - 62
2.	Dr. S. Radhakrishnan	1962 - 67
3.	Dr. Zakir Hussain (expired during the tenure)	1967 - 69
4.	V. V. Giri	1969 - 74
5.	Fakhrudin Ali Ahmed (expired during the tenure)	1974 - 77
6.	N. Sanjeeva Reddy	1977 - 82
7.	Gyani Zail Singh	1982 - 87
8.	R. Venkataraman	1987 - 92

9.	Dr. Shankar Dayal Sharma	1992 - 97
10.	K.R. Narayanan	1997 -

Acting Presidents of India

1.	V. V. Giri (Vice-President)	May - July 1969
2.	Md. Hidayathulla (Chief Justice)	July - Aug. 1969
3.	B.D. Jatti (Vice-President)	Feb. - July 1977

26. VICE - PRESIDENT OF INDIA

1.	**Second in hierarchy**	Vice-President
2.	**Elected by**	Electoral college
3.	**Electoral college**	Members of Lok Sabha and Rajya Sabha
4.	**Term**	5 years
5.	**Duties**	1. (Ex-officio) chairman Rajya Sabha 2. To act as President, during President's absence (1) event of illness (2) death till a new President is elected
6.	**Salary**	Rs. 5,500 p.m. revised at Rs. 14,500 p.m. From 1.1.96 revised at Rs. 40,000/- p.m.
7.	**Pension**	Rs. 6250/- p.m. revised from 28.5.97 to Rs. 20,000 p.m.

Vice-Presidents of India

1.	Dr. S. Radhakrishnan	1952 - 1962
2.	Dr. Zakir Hussain	1962 - 1967
3.	V. V. Giri (resigned)	1967 - 1969
4.	G.S. Pathak	1969 - 1974
5.	B. D. Jatti	1974 - 1979
6.	Md. Hidayathulla (Justice)	1979 - 1984
7.	R. Venkataraman (resigned)	1984 - 1987

8.	Dr. S. D. Sharma	1987 - 1992
9.	K. R. Narayanan	1992 - 1997
10.	Krishna Kant	1997 -

27. PRIME MINISTER

1.	Head of the Council of Ministers	Prime Minister.
2.	Eligibility	Member of Parliament, Leader of a party or parties having the support of the majority of members of Lok Sabha.
3.	Appointed by	President of India.
4.	Tenure	During the pleasure of the President (or) till he enjoys the support of majority in Lok Sabha.
5.	Duties	1. To preside over cabinet meetings
		2. As head of Council of Ministers, to aid and advise President.

PRIME MINISTERS

1.	Jawaharlal Nehru	Aug. 1947 to May '64
2.	Gulzari Lal Nanda (Acting)	May 27th 1964 to June '64
3.	Lal Bahadur Sastri	June 1964 to Jan. '66
4.	Gulzari Lal Nanda (Acting)	Jan. 11th 1966 to 24th Jan. '66
5.	Indira Gandhi	Jan. 1966 to March '77
6.	Morarji Desai	March 1977 to July '79
7.	Charan Singh	July 1979 to Jan. '80
8.	Indira Gandhi	Jan. 1980 to Oct. '84
9.	Rajiv Gandhi	Nov. 1984 to Nov. '89
10.	V. P. Singh	Dec. 1989 to Nov. '90
11.	Chandrasekhar	Nov. 1990 to June '91

12.	P. V. Narasimha Rao	June 1991 to May '96
13.	A. B. Vajpayee	May 1996 (2 weeks)
14.	H. D. Deve Gowda	June 1996 to April '97
15.	I. K. Gujral	April 1997 to March '98
16.	A. B. Vajpayee	March 1998 to April '99
17.	A. B. Vajpayee	Oct. 1999 to

28. CABINET

1.	**Cabinet consists of**	Prime Minister and Cabinet Ministers
2.	**Duties**	1. To aid and advise the President
		2. To decide and determine all government policies
3.	**Responsibility**	Collective responsibility to Parliament
4.	**Departments Dealt with**	1. Cabinet affairs
		2. Personnel
		3. Statistics
5.	**Chief Executive of Cabinet**	Cabinet Secretary Rs.30,000/- p.m. from 1.1.96

COUNCIL OF MINISTERS

1.	Head of the Council of Ministers	**Prime Minister**
2.	Members of Cabinet	**Cabinet Ministers**
3.	Members of Council	**Ministers of State Deputy Ministers**
4.	Appointed by	**The President of India on the advice of the Prime Minister**
5.	Tenure	**During the pleasure of the President**

29. CENTRAL MINISTRIES

1. Agriculture
2. Chemicals & Fertilizers
3. Civil aviation
4. Commerce
5. Communications
6. Defence
7. Energy
8. External Affairs
9. Finance; (Revenue, Expenditure, Banking)
10. Food and Civil Supplies
11. Forest and Environment
12. Health and Family Welfare
13. Home
14. Human Resource Development, Education, Culture, Youth Affairs and Sports
15. Industries (Industrial Development & Internal Trade)
16. Information and Broadcasting
17. Labour Employment and Rehabilitation
18. Law, Justice and Company Affairs
19. Parliamentary Affairs
20. Planning
21. Railways
22. Science and Technology (Atomic Energy, Space, Electronics, Information Technology etc.)
23. Steel, Mines and Coal
24. Surface Transport
25. Textiles
26. Tourism
27. Water Resource and Development
28. Welfare
29. Works, Housing and Urban Development

29-A. CENTRAL GOVERNMENT EMPLOYEES

1. Total no. of Central Government employees   37.2 lakhs
2. Total no. of public sector undertaking employees   35   lakhs
3. Pay and allowances spent per annum   31.066 crores
4. No. of Secretaries and Addl. Secretary officers   258
5. No. of Joint Secretary rank level officers   477
6. No. of Director rank level officers   487

30. PARLIAMENT (Sansad)

1.	**Consists of two Houses**	1. Lok Sabha
		2. Rajya Sabha
2.	**Presiding officers: Lok Sabha**	Speaker, Dy. Speaker
	Elected by	Members of Lok Sabha
3.	**Presiding officers: Rajya Sabha**	Chairman, Dy. Chairman
	Chairman	(Ex. officio) Vice-President
	Deputy Chairman	Elected by Members of Rajya Sabha
4.	**Secretariat**	1. Lok Sabha
		2. Rajya Sabha
5.	**Chief Executives**	Secretary Generals

Lok Sabha

1.	Members Total Stength	**545 (No. of representation in Lok Sabha on the basis of 1971 Census to continue for 25 years from 2001 to 2026.**
2.	Elected by	**Adult Voters in Territorial Constituencies**
3.	Total Constituencies	**543**
	a) General	**423**
	b) Scheduled Caste	**79**
	c) Scheduled Tribes	**41**
4.	Term	**Five years**
5.	Eligibility to become Members	**Indian citizen, 25 years of age, Registered voters**
6.	Nominated Members	
	Anglo-Indians	**2**
7.	Nominated by	**The President of India**
8.	Salary (p.m.)	**Rs. 12,000/-**
	a) D. A. during Session	**Rs. 500/- per day**
	b) Perks	**Rail pass, free telephone, etc.**

Rajya Sabha

1.	**Members Total Stength**	250
2.	**Elected (238 Members) by**	Legislators in the State and Territories
3.	**Nominated Members**	12
4.	**Nominated by**	The President of India
5.	**Term**	6 years; one-third of members retiring every two years
6.	**Eligibility**	Indian citizen, resident of the State (seeking election) 30 years of age
7.	**Salary p.m.**	Rs. 12,000/-
	1. **D.A. per day**	Rs. 500/- During Session
	2. **Perks**	Rail pass, free telephone, etc.

Lok Sabha Periods

S.No.	L. S. No.	From	To	Remark
1.	1st L.S.	17.04.1952	04.04.1957	
2.	2nd L.S.	05.04.1957	31.03.1962	
3.	3rd L.S.	02.04.1962	03.03.1967	
4.	4th L.S.	04.03.1967	27.12.1970	Dissolved
5.	5th L.S.	15.03.1971	18.01.1977	
6.	6th L.S.	23.03.1977	22.08.1979	Dissolved
7.	7th L.S.	10.01.1980	31.12.1984	
8.	8th L.S.	31.12.1984	27.11.1989	
9.	9th L.S.	02.12.1989	13.03.1991	Dissolved
10.	10th L.S.	20.06.1991	14.05.1996	
11.	11th L.S.	15.05.1996	04.12.1997	Dissolved
12.	12th L.S.	12.03.1998	26.04.1999	Dissolved
13.	13th L.S.	20.10.1999		

Lok Sabha - Speakers

S.No.	L. S. No	Period	Speakers
1.	1st L.S.	1947 - 52	G.V. Mavlankar
2.	2nd L.S.	1952 - 56	G.V. Mavlankar (Died)

		1956 - 62	M. Ananthasayanam Iyengar
3.	3rd L.S.	1962 - 67	Sardar Hukham Singh
4.	4th L.S.	1967 - 69	N. Sanjeeva Reddy *(Resigned)*
		1969 - 71	G.S. Dhillon
5.	5th L.S.	1971 - 75	G.S. Dhillon *(Died)*
		1976 - 77	Baliram Bhagath
6.	6th L.S.	1977 - 77	N. Sanjeeva Reddy *(Resigned)*
		1977 - 80	K.S. Hegde
7.	7th L.S.	1980 - 85	Balram Jakhar
8.	8th L.S	1985 - 89	Balram Jakhar
9.	9th L.S.	1989 - 91	Rabi Rai
10.	10th L.S.	1991 - 96	Sivaraj Patil
11.	11th L.S.	1996 - 98	P.A. Sangma
12.	12th L.S.	1998 - 99	G.M.C. Balayogi
13.	13th L.S.	1999 -	G.M.C. Balayogi

31. FINANCE COMMISSION

(Chairman & 4 Members)

S.No.	Year	Commission	Chairman
1.	1953	First	K.C. Neogi
2.	1957	Second	K. Santhanam
3.	1961	Third	K.K. Chanda
4.	1965	Fourth	P.V. Rajamannar
5.	1969	Fifth	Maha Vir Thiagi
6.	1973	Sixth	Brahmananda Reddy
7.	1978	Seventh	J.M. Shelot
8.	1983	Eighth	Y.B. Chavan
9.	1988	Ninth	N.K.P. Salve
10.	1993	Tenth	K.C. Pant
11.	1998	Eleventh	A.N. Khusroo

32. CITIZENSHIP

1. **By Birth**   Every one born in India on or after 26th January 1950.

2.	**By Descent**	If his/her father happened to be a citizen of India at the time of his/her birth.
3.	**Naturalisation**	1. Person of Indian origin living outside India.
		2. Woman married to citizen of India.
		3. Minor children of persons who are citizens of India.
		4. Persons of other countries fulfilling certain conditions can become citizens of India.

33. POLITICAL PARTIES

Recognition	
1. **National Party with common symbol, in all States**	1. If recognised as a party in 3 States.
	2. If a party gets 4% of the total seats of Parliament, even if there is no MLAs in the State.
2. **State Party**	1. If a party gets 6% of the total votes polled in a State, even if there is no MLA elected.
	2. If a party gets 30% of MLAs in the Assembly even if it does not get 6% of the votes polled in the election.

Political Parties

Indian National Congress which struggled for Indian Independence under Mahatma Gandhi, was the only party well known at the time of Independence. Communist party was in existence at that time. In 1964, Communist party was split; Marxists found a separate party.

Rajaji founded a new party in 1959 called Swatantra Party. It failed miserably in 1972 general elections. After the death of Jawaharlal Nehru, Congress party faded. Many breakaway parties formed. It encouraged and enriched local parties at State level.

At National level, besides Congress, Communist and Bharathiya Janatha parties are thriving.

34. JUDICIARY

Supreme Court		
1.	Apex Court	Supreme Court
2.	Judges	Chief Justice and 25 Judges
3.	Appointed by	The President of India
4.	Term	Upto the age of 65 years
5.	Jurisdiction	Federal
	a) Original	Dispute between Union and States and between States
	b) Appellate	Appeal against the judgement of High Courts in India
6.	Functions	To guard the Constitution; to enforce law declared by it
7.		When called for by the President of India, the court is to give opinion
8.	Salary per month:	
	Chief Justice	Rs.10,000/- p.m. revised from 01.01.96, Rs. 33,000/- p.m.
	Judges	Rs.9,000/- p.m. revised from 01.01.96, Rs.30,000/- p.m.
9.	Chief Executive	Registrar-general

Chief Justices of India

S.No.	Name	Date of Assumption
1.	H. J. Kania	26.01.1950
2.	Patanjali Sastry	07.11.1951
3.	M.C. Mahajan	04.01.1954

4.	B.K.Mukerjea	23.12.1954
5.	S.R. Das	02.02.1956
6.	B.P. Sinha	01.10.1959
7.	P.B. Gajendra Gadkhar	01.02.1964
8.	A.K. Sarkar	16.03.1966
9.	K. Subba Rao	30.06.1966
10.	K.N. Wanchoo	12.04.1967
11.	M. Hidayathulla	25.02.1968
12.	J.C.Sha	18.12.1970
13.	S.M. Sikri	23.01.1971
14.	A.N. Ray	27.04.1973
15.	M.H. Baig	28.01.1977
16.	Y.V. Chandrachud	23.02.1978
17.	P.N. Bagavathi	12.07.1985
18.	R.S. Pathak	21.12.1986
19.	E.S. Venkataramiah	19.06.1989
20.	S. Mukerjee	18.12.1989
21.	Ranganath Mishra	25.09.1990
22.	K.N. Singh	26.11.1991
23.	M.H. Kaniah	13.12.1991
24.	L.M. Sharma	18.11.1992
25.	M.N. Venkatachaliah	12.02.1993
26.	A.M. Ahmad	25.10.1994
27.	J.S. Verma	25.03.1997
28.	M.M. Punchi	18.01.1998
29.	A.S. Anand	10.10.1998
30.	S.P. Bharucha	01.11.2001

35. ELECTION COMMISSION

Constitution, Duties & Power

1.	Election Commission	**Chief Election Commissioner and two Commissioners**
2.	Appointed by	**The President of India**
3.	Tenure	**Six years or till the age of 65 years**

4.	Status	**Supreme Court Judge**
5.	Duties	**The superintendence, direction and control and the preparation of electoral rolls and conduct of elections to Parliament, Legislature of states, the President, Vice-President.**
6.	Not eligible	**Re-appointment in Union or States**
7.	Salary for C.E.C.	**Rs. 30,000 p.m.**
	Salary for other Commissioners	**Rs. 26,000 p.m.**

36. ACCOUNTS & AUDIT

Comptroller and Auditor-General

1.	**Head of Accounts and Audit Dept.**	Comptroller and Auditor-General of India
2.	**Appointed by**	The President of India
3.	**Term**	Six years (or) till the age of 65 years whichever is earlier
4.	**Duties and Powers**	1. To audit the accounts of the Union and States
		2. To send report to the President relating to the accounts of the Union to be laid before the Parliament
		3. To send the report of Audit, relating to the State accounts, to the Governors of the State to be laid before the Legislature
5.	**Salary per month**	Rs. 30,000/- (from 1.1.96)
6.	**Status**	Supreme Court Judge
7.	**Not eligible for**	Re-appointment in any office of profit under Union or State Government

37. PUBLIC SERVICE COMMISSION

Constitution

1. Union Public Service Commission	**Chairman and Members**
2. Appointed by	**The President of India**
3. Tenure	**Six years or till the age of 65 years whichever is earlier**
4. Duties	**1. To conduct examinations for appointment under Union Government Service**
Advice	**2. To advise on Service matters consulted by the President of India**
Consultation	**3. Any matters referred to by Union Government regarding recruitment, promotion, disciplinary action etc.**
5. Salaries: Chairman	**Rs. 30,000/ p.m.**
Members	**Rs. 26,000/ p.m.**
6. Not eligible for	**Re-appointment in any office under Union or State Government**

38. VIGILANCE COMMISSION

Central Vigilance Commissioner

1. Central Vigilance Commission	
a) Chairperson	Central Vigilance Commissioner
b) Members	Not more than four commissioners
2. Tenure	
a) Chairperson	4 years / till the age of attaining 65 years
b) Members	3 years / till the age of attaining 65 years

31

3.	**Appointed by**	The President of India
4.	**Selection Committee**	1. Prime Minister (Chairman) 2. Home Minister 3. Leader of opposition in Lok Sabha
5.	**Powers**	1. To probe corruption cases against public servants of Union Government and other Central Service Authorities 2. To select Chief of C.B.I. and E.D. (autonomous status)
6.	**Salary**	
	a) Chairperson	Rs.30,000/- p.m.
	b) Members	Rs.26,000/- p.m.
7.	**Not eligible for**	Re-appointment or employment in any office of profit under Union or State Government

39. LAW OFFICER

Attorney-general of India

1.	Chief Legal officer	**Attorney-general of India**
2.	Appointed by	**The President of India**
3.	Qualification	**Qualified to be appointed as a Judge of Supreme Court**
4.	Duties	**1. To advise the President on legal matters**
		2. To perform duties of legal character
		3. To speak and take part in proceedings of the Parliament and Parliamentary Committee (not entitled to vote)
		4. Right of audience in all courts in the Indian Union

| 5. | Tenure | During the pleasure of the President |

40. NATIONAL HUMAN RIGHTS COMMISSION

1.	**Headquarters**	Delhi
2.	**Chairman**	Former Chief Justice of India
	Members	1. Former Judge of Supreme Court
		2. Former C.J. of High Court
		3. & 4. Human Rights experts
	a) Ex.-officio Members	5. Chairman, National Commission of Minorities
		6. Chairman, National Commission of Scheduled Castes and Tribes
		7. Chairman, National Commission of Women
3.	**Appointed by**	The President of India
4.	**Term**	5 years
5.	**Selection Committee**	1. Speaker, Lok Sabha
		2. Dy. Chairman, Rajya Sabha
		3. Opposition Leader, Lok Sabha
		4. Opposition Leader, Rajya Sabha
6.	Secretary-general	Chief Executive Officer

41. NATIONAL JUDICIAL ACADEMY

Constitution

1.	Governing Council of the Academy	
	Chairman	Chief Justice of India
	Members	1. Supreme Court Judge
		2. Chief Justice of Bombay High Court

		3. Judge of Allahabad High Court
b)	Member of Council Ex.-officio	Secretaries of the Dept. of
		4. Legal Affairs
		5. Justice
		6. Expenditure
2.	Secretary of the Council	Registrar-general of Supreme Court

Functions	
1. **Aims and objects**	1. Training Judicial Officers of States & Territories
	2. Study Court Management and Administration of Justice
	3. Making suggestions for improving Judicial Administration

42. PRESS COUNCIL OF INDIA

Constitution	
1. Constitution	**Press Council Act, 1978**
2. Consists of	**Chairman and 28 Members**
Chairman	**A Retd. Judge of the Supreme Court**
Members	**20 Members from News Paper World. 5 M.Ps., and One each from Sahitya Academy, Bar Council of India, and University Grants Commission.**
3. Functions	**1. To safeguard Freedom of Press**
	2. To improve standard of Newspapers and Agencies
4. Term	**3 years**
5. First Hindi Quarterly published by council	**"Press Parishad Samiksha", September, 1999.**

Part-II ↓ # 1. INDIAN STATES

Constitutional Authorities

1.	State Executive	Governor
	a) Territory Executive	Lt. Governor
2.	State Judiciary	High Court
3.	Public Service	Public Service Commission
4.	Election Commission	State Election Commission
5.	Law Officer	Advocate General

2. STATE EXECUTIVE

Governor

1.	Head of the State	**Governor**
2.	Appointed by	**The President of India**
3.	Qualification	**1. Citizen of India**
		2. Completed 35 years age
		3. Not be a member of Parliament or Legislature of a State
		4. Shall not hold any other office of profit
4.	Term	**Five years**
5.	Residence	**Raj Bhavan at the State Capital**
6.	Powers	
	a) Executive	**All executive actions are expressed in the name of the Governor**
	b) Legislative	**1. He can summon, prorogue, dissolve State Legislature**
		2. To address the House of Legislature, to inaugurate the session
		3. Assent given by the Governor becomes Law
	c) Financial	**1. No money Bill or Financial Bill can be introduced in the Assembly without recommendation of the Governor**

	d) Judicial	Power to pardon, commute or suspend sentence of any person convicted of any offence against the law
6.	Salary per month	Rs. 10,000 with allowances Rs. 36,000 (revised from 1.1.96)

3. STATE JUDICIARY

HIGH COURT

1.	**High Court**	Chief Justice and Judges
2.	**Appointed by**	The President of India
3.	**Term**	Till the age of 62 years
4.	**Jurisdiction**	One or more States / Territories
5.	**Powers**	
	Original	Between State and Citizens
	Appellate	Against the judgement of subordinate courts
6.	**Guardian of the Constitution**	Enforcement of law declared by it
7.	**Salary per month**	Rs. 9000/-
	Chief Justice	revised from 1.1.96, Rs. 30,000
	Judges	Rs. 8000/- revised from 1.1.96, Rs. 26,000
8.	**Total no. of Judges in all High Courts of India**	647

STATE ADMINISTRATIVE TRIBUNAL

1.	Chairman (cadre)	**High Court Judge**
	Vice-chairman (cadre)	**Dt. Judge**
	Member	**Administrative Service Member**
2.	Term	**5 years (or) 62 years**
3.	Appointed by	**Governor of the State**
4.	Juisdiction Original	**Between State and State Service personnel**
5.	Salary (Chairman)	**Rs. 26,000/- p.m.**

HIGH COURTS IN INDIA

Place	Jurisdiction
1. Allahabad H.C (1866) Bench : Lucknow	Uttar Pradesh
2. Bangalore H.C. (1884)	Karnataka
3. Bombay H.C. (1861) Bench : Aurangabad Nagpur	Maharashtra and Dadra Nagar Haveli
Goa	Goa
4. Calcutta H.C. (1861)	West Bengal, Andaman & Nicobar Islands
5. Chandigarh H.C. (1947)	Haryana & Punjab and Chandigarh
6. Cuttack H.C. (1948)	Orissa
7. Gangtok (H.C) 1975	Sikkim
8. Guwahati (1972)	Assam & N.E. States
9. Hyderabad (1956)	Andhra Pradesh
10. Jabalpur H.C. (1956) Bench : Bhopal : Indore : Gwalior	Madhya Pradesh
11. Jodhpur H.C. (1949) Bench : Jaipur	Rajasthan
12. Kochi H.C. (1956)	Kerala & Lakshadweep
13. Madras H.C. (1861) Bench : Madurai	Tamil Nadu & Pondicherry
14. Nainital (2000)	Uttaranchal
15. New Delhi (1966)	Delhi State
16. Patna H.C. (1916)	Bihar
17. Raipur (2000)	Chhattisgarh
18. Rajkot H.C. (1966)	Gujarat
19. Ranchi (2000)	Jharkhand
20. Simla (1971)	Himachal Pradesh
21. Srinagar (1928)	Jammu & Kashmir

4. STATE PUBLIC SERVICE COMMISSION

1.	State Public Service Commission	**Chairman and Members**
2.	Appointed by	**The Governor of the State**
3.	Tenure	**Six years or Sixty-two years of age whichever is earlier**
4.	Qualification	**Must have held office for atleast ten years under Union or State Government**
5.	Duties	**To conduct examinations for appointment under State Government Service**
	Consultation	**To advise on service matters consulted by the Governor of the State regarding recruitment, promotion, disciplinary action referred to by State Government**
6.	Salaries: Chairman	**Rs. 26,000/- p.m.**
7.	Not eligible for	**Re-appointment in any office under Union or State Government**

5. STATE ELECTION COMMISSION

1.	**State Election Commission**	State Election Commissioner
2.	**Appointed by**	The Governor of the State
3.	**Tenure**	Upto the age of 62 years
4.	**Status**	High Court Judge
5.	**Duties**	To supervise, direct, and control electoral process. Preparation of electoral rolls to conduct elections to Local Bodies in the State
6.	**Not eligible**	Re-appointment under Union or State Government
7.	**Salary**	Rs. 26,000 p.m.

6. STATE LAW OFFICER

Advocate-General of the State

1. **Chief Legal officer**	Advocate-General of the State
2. **Appointed by**	The Governor of the State
3. **Qualification**	Qualified to be appointed as judge of the High Court
4. **Duties**	1. To advise the Governor on legal matters
	2. To perform duties of legal character
	3. To speak and take part in the proceedings of the State Assembly, on Committee meetings but not entitled to vote
5. **Right of Audience**	In all courts in the State
6. **Tenure**	During the pleasure of the Governor

7. PARLIAMENTARY COMMITTEES

Select Committee: Select committees are appointed on individual Bills and for making some investigation, inquiry or compilation.

Joint Committee: Joint Committees save time and help to develop bring about good understanding, appreciative spirit and co-operation between the representatives of both houses. To avoid duplication of proceedings, a Bill may be referred to a Joint Committee.

The Estimates Committee: It exercises control over Finance.

The Public Accounts Committee: The function of the Committee is to scrutinize the public accounts and the Report of the Comptroller and Auditor-General of India.

The Committee on Public Undertakings: Its duty is to investigate into the working of Public Undertakings.

Adhoc Committee: Constituted by Speaker or Chairman to inquire into and report on specific subjects (2) To consider and report on a particular Bill.

Part-III ▼

1. DEFENCE SERVICES

1.	Supreme Commander	The President of India
2.	Chief of Defence Staff	Seniormost triservices chief
	(a) Duties	Adviser to Government
	(b) Commander of	Nuclear Assets
3.	Chief of Army Staff	General
4.	Chief of Naval Staff	Admiral
5.	Chief of Air Staff	Air Chief Marshal
	Salary per month	Rs. 33,000/-

Chief of Staff	First Indian
1. Army	Gen. K.M. Kariappa 15.1.49
2. Navy	R.D. Katari 22.4.58
3. Air Force	Surbroto Mukerjee 1.4.54

2. INDIAN ARMY

(Army Day - 15th January)

1.	Headquarters	Delhi
2.	Chief of Army Staff	General
3.	Vice-Chief	Lt. General
4.	Deputy Chief-2	Maj. General
5.	Adjutant General	Maj. General
6.	Quarter Master-general	Maj. General
7.	Master-general of Ordnance	Maj. General
8.	Military Secretary	Maj. General
9.	Engineer-in-Chief	Maj. General

Army Command

1.	Demarcated Geographical Area	Command - 5
2.	Command G.O.C. in Chief	Lieut. General
	a) Northern Command	Udhampur (J. & K.)
	b) Central Command	Lucknow
	c) Southern Command	Pune
	d) Eastern Command	Kolkata
	e) Western Command	Chandigarh
	f) Training Command	Simla

Commands and Corps

1. Commands divided into	**Areas**
Areas divided into	**Sub-areas**
a) Area, G.O.C.	**Major General**
b) Sub-Area O.C.	**Brigadier**
2. Field formations	**Corps**
Corps divided into	**Division**
Divisions divided into	**Brigade**
3. a) Corps Commander	**Lieut.-General**
b) Division Commander	**Major General**
c) Brigade Commander	**Brigadier**

Army Station

4. Army Station Officer Commanding	**Brigadier**
a) Battalion O.C.	**Colonel**
b) Company O.C.	**Major/Captain**
5. Man Power 1990	**12,00,000**
6. Battle Tanks	**3,150**

Indian Army

Corps and Arms

1. Armoured Corps
2. Army Dental Corps
3. Army Education Corps
4. Army Medical Corps
5. Army Ordnance Corps
6. Army Physical Training Corps
7. Army Postal Service Corps
8. Army Supply Corps
9. Corps of Electrical and Mechanical Engineers
10. Corps of Engineers
11. Corps of Signal
12. Defence Sentry Corps

13. Infantry
14. Intelligence Corps of Military Police
15. Military Farm Services
16. Military Nursing Corps
17. Pioneer Corps
18. Regiment of Artillery
19. Remount Veterinary Corps
20. President Bodyguard

Army Institutes

1.	Sainik Schools upto +2 Level	**18 places in India**
2.	Rashtriya Indian Military College (prepare for entrance to N.D.A)	**Dehradun**
3.	National Defence Academy (three services)	**Khadakwasla, Pune**
4.	Indian Military Academy (Army)	**Dehradun**
5.	Officers Training Academy (3 services) Short Courses	**Chennai**
6.	National Defence College	**New Delhi**
7.	The College of Combat	**Mhow**
8.	The College of Military Engineering	**Kirkee**
9.	Military College of Telecommunication Engineering	**Mhow**
10.	The armoured Corps Centre and School	**Ahmed Nagar**
11.	The School Artillery	**Deolali**
12.	The Infantry School	**Mhow and Belgaum**
13.	College of Material Management	**Jabalpur**

Army Commissioned Ranks

1. General
2. Lieutenant General
3. Major General
4. Brigadier
5. Colonel
6. Lt. Colonel

7.	Major	8.	Captain
9.	Lieutenant	10.	Second Lieutenant

Junior Commissioned Officer

1. Subedar - Major
2. Subedar
3. Jamedar

3. INDIAN NAVY

Navy Day - 4th December

1.	Headquarters	**Delhi**
2.	Chief of Naval Staff	**Admiral**
3.	Vice-Chief	**Vice-Admiral**
4.	Deputy Chief	**Rear Admiral**
5.	Chief of Personnel	**Rear Admiral**
6.	Chief of Materials	**Rear Admiral**
7.	Controller of Logistic Support	**Rear Admiral**
8.	Controller of Warship Production & Acquisition	**Rear Admiral**

Naval Command

1. **Naval Commands** 4
2. **Command (F.O.C. in C) Flag Officer Commanding-in-chief** Vice-Admiral
   - a) **Western Command** Mumbai
   - b) **Eastern Command** Vishakapatnam
   - c) **Southern Command** Kochi
   - d) **Far Eastern Command** Andaman
   - e) **Major Naval Bases** Mumbai
     Vishakhapatnam

Naval Establishments

1. **Naval Stations**
   Flag Officer **Commodore**

2. **Naval Stations**

a)	I N S Shivaji	**Lonavla**
b)	I N S Valsura	**Jamnagar**
c)	I N S Chilka	**Bhubaneshwar**
d)	I N S Hansa	**Goa**
e)	I N S Satavahana	**Vishakhapatnam**
f)	I N S Kunjali	**Mumbai**
g)	I N S Ashwini	**Mumbai**
h)	I N S Hamla	**Monva Malad (Mumbai)**
i)	I N S Agrani	**Coimbatore**

1.	Naval Academy	**Goa**
2.	College of Naval Warfare	**Mumbai**
3.	College of Shipwright School	**Vishakhapatnam**

Indian Navy

1.	**Naval Fleets - 2**	Western Fleet
		Eastern Fleet
2.	**Flag officer commanding**	Rear Admiral
3.	**INDIAN NAVAL Ships**	Flag Officer
4.	**Aircraft carrier - 3**	I N S Mysore
		I N S Viraat
		I N S Utkrosh
5.	**Destroyers**	5
	Frigates	18
	Mine Sweepers	20
	Anti Submarines	6
	Submarines	15
	Corvettes Gun Boats	17
	Missile Craft	6
	Jets	68
	Helicopters	75
	Manpower (1995)	52,453

Indian Navy

Commissioned Ranks

1. Admiral
2. Vice-Admiral
3. Rear Admiral
4. Commodore
5. Captain
6. Commander
7. Lieut. Commander
8. Lieutenant
9. Sub Lieutenant
10. Acting Sub-Lieutenant

Junior Commissioned Ranks

1. Master Chief Petty Officer
2. Chief Petty Officer
3. Petty Officer

4. COAST GUARD

1. **Independent Armed Force**   1978
2. **Headquarters**   New Delhi
3. **Head of the coast guard**   Director General (Vice-Admiral)
4. **Regions – 3**   Mumbai, Chennai, Port Blair
   Coast Guard Inspector General   Rear Admiral
5. **Districts of C.G – 11**   Commodore
   1. Vishakhapatnam
   2. Chennai
   3. Haldia
   4. Paradeep
   5. Mumbai
   6. Kandla
   7. Marmugao
   8. Mangalore
   9. Kochi
   10. Diglipur
   11. Campbell Bay

4

5.	**Coast guard Air stations**	1. Mandapam, 2. Tuticorin
6.	**Coast guard Ships**	1. Varaha, 2. Varad
	Commander	Commodore
7.	**Air Squadron, Chennai**	
	Commanding Officer	Lieutenant Commander
◆◦	**Patrol crafts - 51**	
8.	**Duties**	1. To ensure safety and protection of offshore installations
		2. To safeguard Maritime environment from pollution

5. AIR FORCE

Air Force Day - 8th October

1.	**Headquarters**	Delhi
2.	**Chief of Air staff**	Air Chief Marshal
3.	**Vice-chief**	Air Marshal
4.	**Deputy-chief**	Air - Vice Marshal
5.	**Air Officer in-charge Administration**	Air - Vice Marshal
6.	**A.O. in-charge Maintenance**	Air - Vice Marshal
7.	**A.O. in-charge Personnel & Training**	Air - Vice Marshal
8.	**I. G. Flight Safety and Inspection**	Air - Vice Marshal
9.	**Asst. Chief of A.S - 6**	Air Commodore

Air Commands (Estd. 1932)

1.	Demarcated Geographical Area	**Air Command**
2.	Air Commands	**5**
3.	Air officer in chief	**Marshal**
4.	Western Air Command	**Delhi**
5.	S.W. Air Command	**Gandhi Nagar**
6.	Central Air Command	**Allahabad**
7.	Southern Air Command	**Thiruvananthapuram**

8. Functional Commands
   a) Maintenance Command   **Nagpur**
      Training Command   **Bangalore**

Air Force Fleets

1. Combat Fleets
   Air Officer Commanding   Air-Vice Marshal
2. Fleets consist of
   a) Group (consists of wings)   Group Captain
   b) Wings (consists of Squadrons)   Wing Commander
   c) Squadrons   Squadron Leader
3. Fighter Interceptors
4. Fighter Bombers
5. Transport Aircrafts
6. Combat Aircrafts - 844

Air Force Stations

1. Air Force Station
   a) Officer Commanding   Air Commodore

Air Force Institutions

1. Air Force Academy   Hyderabad
2. Helicopter Training School   Hakimpet
3. Flying Instructors School   Tambaram, Chennai
4. The College of Air Warfare   Secunderabad
5. Air Force Administrative College   Coimbatore
6. Air Force Technical College   Jalahalli

Indian Air Force
Commissioned Ranks

1. Air Chief Marshal   2. Air Marshal
3. Air Vice Marshal   4. Air Commodore
5. Group Captain   6. Wing commander
7. Squadron Leader   8. Flight Lieutenant
9. Flying Officer   10. Pilot Officer

6. DEFENCE PRODUCTION UNITS

1.	Bharat Dynamites Ltd.	Hyderabad
2.	Praga Tools	Hyderabad
3.	Mishra Dattu Nigam	Hyderabad
4.	Bharat Electronics Ltd.	Bangalore
5.	Bharath Earthmovers Ltd.	Bangalore
6.	Heavy Vehicles Ltd.	Avadi, Chennai
7.	Garden Reach Ship Builders and Engineers Ltd.	Calcutta
8.	Mazagaon Dock	Mumbai
9.	Goa Shipyard	Marmugao
10.	Hindustan Shipyard Ltd.	Vishakhapatnam
11.	Hindustan Aeronautics Ltd.	Bangalore, Hyderabad, Nasik, Koraput, Kanpur, Lucknow

7. DEFENCE SERVICES
(Very Important Events)

1.	First P.V. Chakra awarded posthumously	**Major Somnath Sharma of Indian Army in 1947**
2.	First P.V. Chakra awarded posthumously	**Flying officer, Nirmal Jeet Singh Shekon of Indian Air Force in 1971**
3.	First Indian astronaut aboard the Soviet spacecraft (Soyuz T. 10)	**Sq. Leader Rakesh Sharma of I.A.F. in April 1984**
4.	First Indian to hoist Indian National Flag over North Pole	**Sq. Leader Sanjay Thapar**
5.	First indigenously built submarine commissioned	**I. N.S. Shalki on 7.2.92**
6.	First indigenously built missile destroyer commissioned	**I.N.S. Delhi at Mumbai on 5.11.97**

| 7. | Defence Research and Development Organisation in collaboration with Dept. of Atomic energy conducted | **Five Nuclear underground Tests at Pokhran May 18, in 1974 and again in May 12, 13, 1998** |

8. DECORATION IN DEFENCE FORCES

Awards and Medals

I. GALLANTRY AWARD

    1. Param Vir Chakra (P.V.C.)   2. Maha Vir Chakra (M.V.C.)

    3. Vir Chakra (V.C)   4. Uttam Yuddh Seva Medal

II. GALLANTRY AWARD (Peace Time)

    1. Ashok Chakra   2. Kirthi Chakra

    3. Sourya Chakra   4. Sena Medal

    5. Nao Sena Medal   6. Vayu Sena Medal

III. DISTINGUISHED SERVICE MEDALS

    1. Param Vishist Seva Medal   2. Adi Vishist Seva Medal

    3. Vishist Seva Medal

CHRONOLOGICAL HIGHLIGHTS

1.	**October 1949**	- Territorial Army raised.
2.	**October 26, 1962**	- President promulgates the Defence of India Ordinance.
3.	**August 14, 1963**	- NCC training made compulsory.
4.	**January 10, 1966**	- Tashkent Declaration.
5.	**July 2, 1972**	- 'Simla Agreement' signed between India and Pakistan.
6.	**May 21, 1989**	- Successful launch of 'AGNI' at Chandipur, Orissa.
7.	**June 5, 1989**	- 'Trishul' - India's surface-to-surface missile successfully test-fired.
8.	**March 1, 1993**	- 'Arjun' - India's main battle tank launched.
9.	**May 26, 1999**	- PSLV-C2 launched.
10.	**March 22, 2000**	- INSAT-3B launched.
11.	**April 18, 2001**	- GSLV-D1 launched.

Part-IV ▼

1. STATES IN INDIAN UNION
(Population - 2001)

S.No.	State	Population Crores	Population Growth per 1000
1.	Andhra Pradesh	7.57	21.7
2.	Arunachal Pradesh	1.09	22.3
3.	Assam	2.66	27.0
4.	Bihar	8.28	30.4
5.	Chhattisgarh	2.07	-
6.	Goa	0.13	14.3
7.	Gujarat	5.05	25.4
8.	Haryana	2.10	26.8
9.	Himachal Pradesh	0.60	23.8
10.	Jammu & Kashmir	1.00	-
11.	Jharkhand	2.69	-
12.	Karnataka	5.27	22.3
13.	Kerala	3.18	18.0
14.	Madhya Pradesh	6.03	30.7
15.	Maharashtra	9.67	21.1
16.	Manipur	0.24	18.6
17.	Meghalaya	0.23	28.7
18.	Mizoram	0.08	17.0
19.	Nagaland	0.20	-
20.	Orissa	3.67	24.1
21.	Punjab	2.42	21.5
22.	Rajasthan	5.64	31.1
23.	Sikkim	0.05	21.6
24.	Tamil Nadu	6.21	19.3
25.	Tripura	0.31	17.0
26.	Uttar Pradesh	16.60	32.1
27.	Uttaranchal	0.84	-
28.	West Bengal	8.02	20.7

S.No.	State	Population Crores	Population Growth per 1000
1.	Delhi	1.37	19.4
2.	Andaman & Nicobar Islands	3.56	18.1
3.	Chandigarh	9.00	17.9
3.	Daman & Diu	1.58	26.9
5.	Dadra Nagar Haveli	2.20	32.4
6.	Lakshadweep	0.60	25.1
7.	Pondicherry	9.73	17.7

2. MINERAL WEALTH

	Mineral	States
1.	Bauxite	Andhra Pradesh, Bihar, Goa, Gujarat, Jammu & Kashmir, Karnataka, Kerala, Madhya Pradesh, Maharashtra, Orissa, Rajasthan, Tamil Nadu, Uttar Pradesh
2.	Chromite (Main produce in the world)	Bihar, Karnataka, Orissa Maharashtra, Manipur, Tamil Nadu
3.	Coal	Gondwana (A.P.), Bihar, Madhya Pradesh, Assam, Meghalaya, Nagaland, Jammu & Kashmir
4.	Copper	Andhra Pradesh, Madhya Pradesh, Bihar, Gujarat, Karnataka, Rajasthan
5.	Diamond	Madhya Pradesh, Uttar Pradesh
6.	Gold	Andhra Pradesh, Karnataka
7.	Gypsum	Rajasthan, Tamil Nadu, Jammu & Kashmir
8.	Ilmenite	Kerala, Orissa, Tamil Nadu
9.	Iron ore	Bihar, Goa, Karnataka, Madhya Pradesh, Maharashtra, Orissa, Tamil Nadu

10. **Lead-Zinc**	Gujarat, Rajasthan
11. **Lignite**	Gujarat, Rajasthan, Jammu & Kashmir, Tamil Nadu
12. **Manganese**	Andhra Pradesh, Madhya Pradesh, Goa, Gujarat, Karnataka, Orissa, Maharashtra
13. **Mica** (Main produce in the world)	Andhra Pradesh, Bihar, Rajasthan
14. **Magnesite**	Tamil Nadu, Karnataka, Uttar Pradesh
15. **Rock Salt**	Himachal Pradesh
16. **Salt**	Coastal region of Gujarat, Maharashtra, Tamil Nadu, Rajasthan

CRUDE OIL

Petroleum Occurring States

1. Ganga Valley	2. Punjab
3. Himachal Pradesh	4. Kutch (offshore)
5. West Bengal	6. Orissa
7. Andhra Pradesh	8. Tamil Nadu
9. Karnataka	10. Gujarat
11. Maharashtra	

3. MAJOR INDUSTRIES

Industry	States
1. **Aluminium**	Orissa, Tripura
2. **Automobiles**	Tamil Nadu, Bihar, West Bengal, Haryana
3. **Cement**	Madhya Pradesh, Rajasthan, Andhra Pradesh, Haryana
4. **Chemicals & Fertilisers**	Gujarat and Bihar
5. **Dairy Products**	Gujarat
6. **Electronics**	Uttar Pradesh, Karnataka, Delhi

7.	**Films**	Maharashtra, Uttar Pradesh
8.	**Iron & Steel**	Madhya Pradesh, Bihar, Orissa
9.	**Jute**	West Bengal
10.	**Leather**	Tamil Nadu, Uttar Pradesh, West Bengal
11.	**Machine Tools**	Karnataka, Chandigarh (tractors)
12.	**Marbles**	Rajasthan
13.	**Paper**	Madhya Pradesh, Andhra Pradesh, Orissa, Haryana, Meghalaya
14.	**Petroleum**	Assam
15.	**Rubber**	Kerala, Goa
16.	**Shipbuilding**	Andhra Pradesh, Goa
17.	**Silk**	Jammu & Kashmir
18.	**Sugar**	Maharashtra, Manipur
19.	**Textiles**	Tamil Nadu, Rajasthan, Maharashtra, Gujarat, Punjab, Pondicherry

4. MAIN CROPS

	Crops	Producing States
1.	Barley	**Uttar Pradesh, Rajasthan**
2.	Black Pepper	**Kerala, Karnataka**
3.	Cardamom	**Karnataka, Kerala**
4.	Chilli (Dry)	**Tamil Nadu, Andhra Pradesh**
5.	Coffee	**Karnataka, Kerala**
6.	Coriander	**Rajasthan, Andhra Pradesh**
7.	Cotton	**Gujarat, Maharashtra**
8.	Ginger (Dry)	**Kerala, Himachal Pradesh**
9.	Gram	**Rajasthan, Uttar Pradesh**
10.	Groundnut*	**Gujarat, Tamil Nadu**
11.	Jowar	**Maharashtra, Karnataka**
12.	Jute*	**West Bengal, Bihar**
13.	Linseed	**Madhya Pradesh, Uttar Pradesh**

14. Maize	**Uttar Pradesh, Bihar**
15. Millet (small)*	**Madhya Pradesh, Uttar Pradesh**
16. Pulses	**Rajasthan, Orissa, Madhya Pradesh, Maharashtra**
17. Ragi	**Karnataka, Tamil Nadu**
18. Mustard	**Uttar Pradesh, Rajasthan**
19. Paddy*	**West Bengal, Tamil Nadu**
20. Saffron	**Maharashtra, Karnataka**
21. Sunn hemp	**Uttar Pradesh, Madhya Pradesh**
22. Sesame	**Uttar Pradesh, Rajasthan**
23. Sugarcane	**Uttar Pradesh, Maharashtra**
24. Tapioca	**Kerala, Tamil Nadu**
25. Tea*	**Assam, Kerala, Tamil Nadu**
26. Tobacco	**Maharashtra, Andhra Pradesh**
27. Tur	**Uttar Pradesh, Madhya Pradesh**
28. Wheat*	**Uttar Pradesh, Punjab**

*India is primary producer in the World.

CROP SEASONS

1. **Rabi crops** **Wheat, Grams,** **Linseed, Mustard, etc.**	Sown in October, November
2. **Kharif Crops** **Rice, Millets, Maize,** **Cotton, etc.**	Sown in June

5. HILL STATIONS

1. Almora, Mussoorie Nainital	**Uttaranchal**
2. Cherrapunji (Shillong), Khasi Hills (Shillong)	**Meghalaya**
3. Ooty, Kodaikanal, Yercaud	**Tamil Nadu**

4.	Dalhousie, Kassauli, (Simla)	**Himachal Pradesh**
5.	Darjeeling	**West Bengal**
6.	Gulmarg, Srinagar	**Kashmir**
7.	Mahabaleshwar	**Maharashtra**
8.	Mt. Abu	**Rajasthan**
9.	Pachmarhi	**Madhya Pradesh**
10.	Ranchi	**Jharkhand**

6. NATIONAL PARKS

1.	**Corbett National Park**	Nainital, Uttaranchal
2.	**Dudhwa National Park**	Lakhimpur Kheri, Uttar Pradesh
3.	**Kaziranga National Park**	Jorhat, Assam
4.	**Kanha National Park**	Jabalpur, Bhedaghat
5.	**Gir National Park**	Rajkot, Junagadh, Gujarat
6.	**Guindy National Park**	Guindy, Chennai, Tamil Nadu
7.	**Nagarhole National Park**	Coorg, Karnataka
8.	**Bandipur National Park**	Mysore, Karnataka

NATIONAL WILDLIFE SANCTUARIES

1.	**Dachigam Wildlife Sanctuary**	Srinagar, Jammu & Kashmir
2.	**Sariska**	Alwar, Rajasthan
3.	**Hazaribagh Wildlife Sanctuary**	Hazaribagh, Jharkhand
4.	**Tiger Project**	Sawai Madhopur, Rajasthan
5.	**Mudhumalai Wildlife Sanctuary**	Mudumalai, Nilgiris, Tamil Nadu
6.	**Periyar Wildlife Sanctuary**	Idukki, Kottayam, Kerala

7. HOLY PLACES IN INDIA

1.	**Amarnath**	Kashmir
2.	**Ayodhya**	Uttar Pradesh
3.	**Badrinath**	Uttar Pradesh

4.	**Dwaraka**	Gujarat
5.	**Haridwar**	Uttaranchal
6.	**Kancheepuram**	Tamil Nadu
7.	**Kedarnath**	Uttaranchal
8.	**Mathura**	Uttar Pradesh
9.	**Puri**	Orissa
10.	**Rameswaram**	Tamil Nadu
11.	**Tirupathi**	Andhra Pradesh
12.	**Ujjain**	Madhya Pradesh
13.	**Varanasi**	Uttar Pradesh

8. CULTURAL CENTRES

	Zone	Zonal HQ
1.	Southern Zone	**Thanjavur (Tamil Nadu)**
2.	South Central Zone	**Nagpur (Maharashtra)**
3.	North Zone	**Patiala (Punjab)**
4.	North Cenral Zone	**Allahabad (Uttar Pradesh)**
5.	North Eastern Zone	**Dimapur (Nagaland)**
6.	East Zone	**Kolkata (West Bengal)**
7.	West Zone	**Udaipur (Rajasthan)**

9. POPULAR BEACH RESORTS

1.	**Kovalam**	Kerala
2.	**Juhu**	Mumbai
3.	**Mamallapuram**	Tamil Nadu
4.	**Marina**	Chennai, Tamil Nadu
5.	**Konarak**	Orissa
6.	**Puri**	Orissa
7.	**Waltair**	Andhra Pradesh
8.	**Goa**	Goa

10. SCIENCE AND TECHNOLOGY

1.	**Department of Space**	Satellite operations and Development
2.	**Department of Science and Technology**	Research and Development of Robotics; climate, Neuro science, seismological study

3.	**Department of Ocean Development**	Generation of electricity from sea waves, desalination, pollution monitoring, aquaculture farming, fisheries development, research in Antarctica
4.	**Department of Electronics**	Micro electronic development Super Computer Development
5.	**Computer Maintenance**	Informative technology for management system, Finger Print Analysis, criminal tracing system
6.	**Department of Bio-technology**	Research and Services in oil palm cultivation, aquaculture, medical plants, neurobiology, biotechnology, biological, pest control

11. INDIAN SPACE RESEARCH ORGANISATIONS

1.	Space Science and Technology (Estd. 1965)	**Centre**
	Equatorial Rocket Launching Station (TERLS)	**Thumba**
2.	Space Application Centre (Estd.1967)	**Ahmedabad**
	Satellite Communication Earth station	
3.	Indian Space Research Organisation (Estd 15.8.69)	**Bangalore**
4.	Space Commission (Estd. 1.6.1972)	**Bangalore**
5.	Indian Scientific Satellite Project	**Bangalore**
6.	Physical Research Laboratory	**Ahmedabad**
7.	Propelling Fuel Complex	**Thiruvananthapuram**
8.	Satellite Launch Vehicle Project	**Thiruvananthapuram**
9.	Vikram Sarabai Space Centre	**Thiruvananthapuram**
10.	Sriharikotta Range	**Sriharikotta, A.P.**

12. SCIENTIFIC AND INDUSTRIAL RESEARCH

1.	**Department of Scientific and Industrial Research**	To encourage industries to use available infrastructure for R & D. requirements
2.	**National Research Development Corporation**	Technological transfer organisation, commercialise indigenously developed technology (low cost heart valve)
3.	**Central Electronics Limited**	Photo Voltare through research and development
4.	**Council of Scientific and Industrial Research**	With network of laboratories spearhead in basic and applied science

13. CIVIL AIRWAYS

(International Airports - 1972)

1.	Santa Cruz	**Mumbai**
2.	Dum Dum	**Kolkata**
3.	Palam (Indira Gandhi Memorial)	**New Delhi**
4.	Anna Terminal	**Chennai**
5.	Raja Sansi Airport	**Amritsar**

14. CIVIL AVIATION

(National Airport Authority 1986)

Domestic Airports - 47

1.	**Agartala**	Tripura
2.	**Agra**	Uttar Pradesh
3.	**Ahmedabad**	Gujarat
4.	**Allahabad**	Uttar Pradesh
5.	**Bangalore**	Karnataka
6.	**Belgaum**	Karnataka

7.	**Bhav Nagar**	Gujarat
8.	**Bhopal**	Madhya Pradesh
9.	**Bhubaneshwar**	Orissa
10.	**Chandigarh**	Chandigarh
11.	**Coimbatore**	Tamil Nadu
12.	**Dehradun**	Uttaranchal
13.	**Dibrugarh**	Assam
14.	**Dimapur**	Nagaland
15.	**Guwahati**	Assam
16.	**Mormugao**	Goa
17.	**Gorakhpur**	Uttar Pradesh
18.	**Gwalior**	Madhya Pradesh
19.	**Hyderabad**	Andhra Pradesh
20.	**Imphal**	Manipur
21.	**Indore**	Madhya Pradesh
22.	**Jaipur**	Rajasthan
23.	**Jammu**	Jammu & Kashmir
24.	**Jodhpur**	Rajasthan
25.	**Jorhat**	Assam
26.	**Kochi**	Kerala
27.	**Lengpui**	Mizoram
28.	**Lucknow**	Uttar Pradesh
29.	**Madurai**	Tamil Nadu
30.	**Mangalore**	Karnataka
31.	**Nainital**	Uttaranchal
32.	**Nagpur**	Maharashtra
33.	**Patna**	Bihar
34.	**Pondicherry City**	Pondicherry
35.	**Port Blair**	Andaman
36.	**Pune**	Maharashtra
37.	**Raipur**	Chhattisgarh
38.	**Ranchi**	Jharkhand
39.	**Silchar**	Assam
40.	**Srinagar**	Jammu & Kashmir
41.	**Tezpur**	Assam
42.	**Tirupathi**	Andhra Pradesh
43.	**Tiruchirapalli**	Tamil Nadu

44. **Thiruvananthapuram**	Kerala
45. **Udaipur**	Rajasthan
46. **Vadodara**	Gujarat
47. **Varanasi**	Uttar Pradesh
48. **Vijayawada**	Andhra Pradesh
49. **Vishakhapatnam**	Andhra Pradesh

15. LIFE INSURANCE CORPORATION OF INDIA

1.	Nationalised on	1.9.1956
	a) Insurance Companies Indian and Foreign Companies	**245**
	b) Central office	**Mumbai**
	c) Zonal office	**Mumbai, Kolkata, Delhi, Chennai, Hyderabad, Kanpur, Bhopal**
	d) Divisional offices	**100**
	e) Branch offices	**2048**
2)	General Insurance Company Nationalised on —	**November, 1972**
	a) Subsidiary Companies Total units	**107 (groups - 4)**
	National Insurance Company Ltd.	**Kolkata**
	New India Assurance Co. Ltd.	**Mumbai**
	Oriental Insurance Co. Ltd.	**New Delhi**
	United India Insurance Co. Ltd.	**Chennai**

16. FOOD CORPORATION OF INDIA

1.	**Established**	1965
	a) Purpose	Storage, distribution protection of the interest of farmers and consumers
	b) Warehousing by	Central Warehousing Corporation, 16 State Warehousing Corporations
	c) March 2000 Warehouses Storage Capacity	456
		251.15 lakh tons

17. OIL CORPORATION

1.	Indian Oil Corporation	Estd. 1964
	a) Amalgamation of	Indian Refineries Ltd. and Indian Oil Company Ltd.
2.	Hindustan Petroleum Corporation	Estd. 1974
	a) Amalgamation of	Assets of ESSO in India
3.	Bharat Petroleum Corporation	Estd. 1976
	Acquisition of	Two Burmah Shell companies

18. INDIAN RAILWAYS

(As on 31.03.1999)

1.	First Rail Service 1853	Bombay to Thane - 35 km
2.	Total route kilometers	62,809 km
3.	Total trains running every day	13,000 trains
4.	First underground rail service	In Kolkata (1984)
5.	Mass Rapid Transport System (elevated Railway)	In Chennai Beach to Tirumylai

Zonal Railways

1.	South Railway	Chennai
2.	South Eastern Railway	Kolkata, Garden Reach
3.	South Central Railway	Secunderabad
4.	South Western Railway	Bangalore
5.	Northern Railway	New Delhi
6.	North Eastern Railway	Gorakhpur
7.	North East Frontier Rly.	Maligaon (Guwahati)
8.	North Western Railway	Jaipur
9.	Western Railway	C.G. Mumbai
10.	West Coast Railway	Jabalpur
11.	Eastern Railway	Kolkata
12.	East Coast Railway	Bhubaneshwar
13.	East Central Railway	Hazipur
14.	Central Railway	Mumbai V.T.
15.	Central East Railway	Bilaspur
	Total no. of Railway Stations	7076
	Total strength of staff	1.65 Millions

5

19. MAJOR PORTS

I. **Western Zone**

1. Mumbai
2. Kandla (1957)
3. Mormugao (1963)
4. New Mangalore (1974)
5. Cochin
6. Jawaharlal Nehru Port, Mumbai (1989)

II. **Eastern Zone**

1. Chennai
2. Vishakapatnam
3. Kolkata-Haldia (1977)
4. Paradeep (1966)
5. Thoothukudi (1974)
6. Ennore (1999)

SHIPPING SERVICES

1.	Indian Coastline	7,516 km
2.	Shipping Companies	102 including S.C.I.
	a) Coastline trade	65
	b) Overseas trade	26
	c) Both trade	11
3.	Shipping Corporation	
	Number of fleets	112 Vessels
	G.R.T. (43% of total)	29.49 lakh
4.	Major Ports	12
5.	Minor Ports	139
6.	Coastal Fleet	274 ships (6,81,762 GRT)

20. POSTAL INDEX NUMBER

Indian Postal Service Commenced on 01.10.1854

1.	110	Delhi
	120	Haryana
	140	Punjab
	160	Chandigarh

	170	Himachal Pradesh
	180	Jammu & Kashmir
2.	200	Uttar Pradesh
3.	300	Rajasthan
	360	Gujarat, Daman, Diu, Dadra and Nagar Haveli
4.	400	Maharashtra
	403	Goa
	450	Madhya Pradesh
5.	500	Andhra Pradesh
	560	Karnataka
6.	600	Tamil Nadu
	670	Kerala, Lakshadweep
7.	700	West Bengal
	750	Orissa
	780	Assam
	790	Andaman & Nicobar, N.E. States
8.	800	Bihar

POSTAL SERVICES

1.	Postal Service commenced	1837
	a) First postage stamp issued at Karachi	1852
2.	Separate Postal Dept. commenced	1854
	a) No. of Post offices (1854)	700
	b) 1st Post card introduced (3 paise)	1879
	c) M.O. introduced	1880
	d) Savings Bank Service	1882
	e) Postal Life Insurance	1884
3.	Postal Mail Service	1907
4.	Air Mail Service	1911
5.	Posts & Telecommunication started	1984
	Total Post Offices (2000)	1,54,149
	Quick Mail Service	1975
	Speed Post	1986

21. TELECOMMUNICATION

1.	Telephone Service introduced in Kolkata	**1881-82**
2.	First automatic exchange commissioned	**1913-14 at Simla**
3.	Total Telephone exchanges in India (March 2000)	**27,909**
	a) Capacity	**32.8 million lines**
	b) Telephones	**26.5 millions**
4.	Maha Nagar Telephone Nigam Ltd. (MTNL) at Mumbai & Delhi	**April 1986**
5.	Videsh Sanchar Nigam Limited (VSNL)	**April 1986**
6.	Bharat Sanchar Nigam launched with functional autonomy on	**01-10-2000**
7.	Total Staff Strength	**10,08,380**

BROADCASTING CORPORATION
22. ALL INDIA RADIO

1.	All India Radio (Private Corporation)	
	a) Established in the year at Bombay & Calcutta	**1927**
2.	First relay started in	**1927, July**
3.	Taken over by Central Government	**1932**
	Known as Akashwani from	**1957**
4.	Total Stations (2000)	**199**

23. DOORDARSHAN (Television)

1.	Doordarshan	**Delhi**
	a) Experimental (First telecast)	**15.9.1959**
	b) T. V. Station at Bombay	**15.9.1972**
	c) T. V. Station at Chennai, Koltaka, Lucknow, Srinagar, Amritsar	**15.9.1974**
2.	18 Stations started to relay	**1979**
3.	11 Stations started to relay	**1986**

4.	Metro channel	1988
5.	Terrestrial telecast at	1993
	5 Places (Regional)	1. **Delhi,**
		2. **Mumbai**
		3. **Kolkata,**
		4. **Chennai**
		5 **Lucknow**

a) Terrestrial Telecast extended to
   10 stations   1994
b) Prasar Bharathi   23.11.1997

DOORDARSHAN CHANNELS
(15.8.1994)

	Channel	**Kendra**	**Subject**
1.	**Primary**	Delhi	Hindi
2.	**Metro**	Delhi	Hindi
3.	**Three**	Delhi	English & Hindi
4.	**Four**	Thiruvananthapuram	Malayalam
5.	**Five**	Chennai	Tamil (Pothigai)
6.	**Six**	Bhubaneshwar	Oriya
7.	**Seven**	Kolkata	Bengali
8.	**Eight**	Hyderabad	Telugu
9.	**Nine**	Bangalore	Kannada
10.	**Ten**	Mumbai	Marathi
11.	**Eleven**	Ahmedabad	Gujarathi
12.	**Twelve**	Jullandar	Punjabi
		Srinagar	Kashmiri
13.	**Thirteen**	Guwahati	Assamese & N. E. languages

24. NATIONAL HIGHWAYS
(N.H. Total 69 - 38517 km)

1.	**N.H. 1**	**Delhi - Chandigarh**, Ludhiana
	456 km	Jullandar, - Amritsar - (A) **Srinagar**

2.	**N.H. 2** 1490 km	**Delhi** - Mathura - **Agra** - Kanpur **Allahabad** - Varanasi - Dhanbad - **Kolkata,** (25) Kanpur - **Lucknow**
3.	**N.H. 3** 1161 km	**Mumbai** - Nasik - Indore - Gwalior - Agra
4.	**N.H. 4** 1235 km	**Mumbai** - Pune - Belgaum - Hubli - **Bangalore** - Chittoor - Ranipet - **Chennai**
	N.H. 4(A)	**Belgaum - Panaji**
5.	**N.H. 5** 1533 km	**Chennai** - Nellore - Vijayawada Vishakapatnam - **Bhubaneshwar -** **Kolkata**
6.	**N.H. 6** 1932 km	**Mumbai** - Nasik - Akola - Nagpur - Raipur - Sambalpur - Karagpur - **Kolkata**
7.	**N.H. 7** 2369 km Longest Road	Varanasi - Jabalpur - Nagpur Adilabad - Nizamabad - **Hyderabad** - Kurnool - Gutty - **Bangalore** - Krishnagiri - Salem - Coimbatore - Dindigul - Madurai - Tirunelveli - **Kanyakumari**
8.	**N.H. 8** 1428 km	**Mumbai** - Surat - Vadodara - Gandhi Nagar - Udaipur - Jodhpur - Ajmer - **Jaipur - Delhi**
9.	**N.H. 9** 791 km	**Mumbai** - Pune - Sholapur - **Hyderabad** - Vijayawada
10.	**N.H. 10** 403 km	**Delhi** - Hissar - Sirsi - Ganga Nagar - (Pak. Border)
11.	**N.H. 11** 582 km	Agra - **Jaipur** - Sikar - Ratanpur - Bikaner
12.	**N.H. 12** 890 km	Ajmer - Kota - **Bhopal** - Jabalpur
13.	**N.H. 13** 491 km	Sholapur - Bijapur - Hospet - Chithra Durga
14.	**N.H. 14** 450 km	Beawar - Sirohi - Radhampur

15.	**N.H. 15** 1526 km	Pathankot - Amritsar - Ganga Nagar - Bikaner - Jaisalmer - Bumer - Khandla
16.	**N.H. 16** (460 km)	Nizamabad - Jagadalpur
17.	**N.H. 17** 1269 km	**Mumbai** - Ratnagiri - **Panaji** - Kunta - Mangalore - Mahe - **Calicut** - Trichur - Cranganur
18.	**N.H. 18** 369 km	Kurnool - Nandyal - Cuddappah
19.	**N.H. 19** 240 km	Ghazipur - Balia - Patna
20.	**N.H. 20** 220 km	Pathankot - Mandi (H.P.)

25. BANKING IN INDIA
RESERVE BANK OF INDIA

1.	**Established**	1935
2.	**Share Capital**	5 Crores (Five Crores)
3.	**Taken over by** **Central Government**	1st January 1949
4.	**Headquarters**	Mumbai
5.	**Branch offices**	1. Ahmedabad 2. Bangalore 3. Bhubaneshwar 4. Kolkata 5. Guwahati 6. Hyderabad 7. Jaipur 8. Kanpur 9. Chennai 10. Mumbai 11. Nagpur 12. New Delhi 13. Patna 14. Thiruvananthapuram
6.	**Represents**	International Monetary Fund
7.	**Functions**	1. To regulate issue of Bank notes 2. To keep reserves for monetary security 3. As a sole authority to issue of currency in India and to undertake distribution

a) **Issue of currency of one rupee and less than one rupee**   By Govt. of India only

8. **Maintenance of**   Exchange value of rupee

9. **Formulation of**   Monetary Policy

10. **Administer Policy over**   Other Banks in India

11. **Bankers to**
   1. Central Government
   2. State Governments in India
   3. Co-operative Banks and
   4. Other Scheduled Banks

26. STATE BANK OF INDIA

1. **Imperial Bank of India**   Taken over by Central Government on 1.7.55

   a) As per Act   State Bank of India Act of 1955

2. **Main Bank**   State Bank of India

   Subsidiaries
   1. **State Bank of Bikaner and Jaipur**
   2. **State Bank of Hyderabad**
   3. **State Bank of Indore**
   4. **State Bank of Mysore**
   5. **State Bank of Patiala**
   6. **State Bank of Saurashtra**
   7. **State Bank of Travancore**

3. Nationalisation of Banks   **14 banks brought under public sector, in July 1969**

27. NATIONALISED BANKS

a) **Nationalised in July 1969**
   1. Bank of Baroda
   2. Bank of India
   3. Central Bank of India
   4. Bank of Maharashtra
   5. Allahabad Bank
   6. Canara Bank

7. Dena Bank
8. Indian Bank
9. Indian Overseas Bank
10. Punjab National Bank
11. Syndicate Bank
12. Union Bank of India
13. United Bank of India
14. United Commercial Bank

4.	**Nationalisation of Bank**	6 banks brought under public sector on 15.4.1980
	a) Nationalised on 15.4.1980	1. Andhra Bank
		2. Corporation Bank
		3. New Bank of India now merged with P.N.B.
		4. Oriental Bank of Commerce
		5. Punjab and Sind Bank
		6. Vijaya Bank
5.	**Scheduled Banks**	Bank with not less than 5 lakh (Five lakh) capital and reserve

28. NATIONAL BANKS (A)

1. **National Bank of Agriculture and Rural Development**

   a) Constituted on   **12.7.1982**

2. Apex Bank   **(for) all matters of Policy planning, operational aspects of flow of credits**

3. Function   **To meet the credit needs of all types of agriculture and rural development activities**

4. To promote rural economic activity
   1. **Agriculture**
   2. **Small scale Industries**
   3. **Cottage and Village industries**
   4. **Handicrafts**
   5. **Rural credit**

NATIONAL BANK (B)

1. **Industrial**   Industrial Reconstuction
   Reconstruction   Bank of India (IRBI)
   a) Constituted in   1984
2. **Offices**   1.   Mumbai
                          2.   Ahmedabad
                          3.   Bhopal
                          4.   Bangalore
                          5.   Guwahati
                          6.   Hyderabad
                          7.   Lucknow
                          8.   Chennai
                          9.   Delhi
                        10. Kolkata

NATIONAL BANK (C)

1. **Industrial**   Industrial Development
   Development   Bank of India (IDBI)
   a) Headquarters   Mumbai
   b) Branches   Mumbai, Kolkata, Guwahati,
                          Chennai, New Delhi.
2. **Functions**   Banks to Industries

NATIONAL BANK (D)

1. **Small Industries** Small Industries Development
   Development   Bank of India (SIDBI)
   a) Headquarters   Mumbai
2. **Functions**   Apex Development Bank for Small
                          Scale Sector

NATIONAL BANK (E)

1. **Export Import**   Export Import Bank of India
   a) Established on 1.1.1982
   b) Headquarters   Mumbai
2. **Branches**   1. New Delhi 2. Kolkata
                        3. Chennai   4. Mumbai
                        5. Bangalore

3.	Functions	To grant deferred payment credit of medium and long-term duration for 1. Export projects 2. Capital goods 3. Engineering goods 4. Consultancy Services
4.	Issues guarantee & participation	(in) consortium with commercial banks

29. STOCK EXCHANGES

1.	Mumbai	2.	Chennai
3.	Coimbatore	4.	Kolkata
5.	New Delhi	6.	Ahmedabad
7.	Vadodara	8.	Rajkot
9.	Kutch	10.	Hyderabad
11.	Bangalore	12.	Mangalore
13.	Hubli – Dharwar	14.	Kochi
15.	Bhubaneshwar	16.	Jaipur
17.	Indore	18.	Kanpur
19.	Ludhiana	20.	Guwahati
21.	Magath (Patna)		

30. ALL INDIA SERVICE

1. **Indian Administrative Service**
2. **Indian Audit and Accounts Service**
3. **Indian Foreign Service**
4. **Indian Forest Service**
5. **Indian Police Service**
6. **Indian Postal Service**
7. **Indian Revenue Service**

31. CENTRAL POLICE FORCE

1. Assam Rifles (AR)
2. Border Security Force (BSF)
3. Central Bureau of Investigation (CBI)
4. Central Industrial Security Force (CISF)

5. Central Reserve Police Force (CRPF)
6. Indo-Tibetan Border Police (ITBP)
7. Special Protection Group (SPG)

INTELLIGENCE FORCE

1. Intelligence Bureau
2. Research and Analysis Wing

ALL INDIA SERVICE - TRAINING INSTITUTION

1. **National Academy of Administration (August-1959)**	Mussoorie
a) To provide	Common foundational course All India and Class I Central Services
2. **School of International Studies, New Delhi**	Course covering to train Indian Foreign Services
3. **School of International Law and Diplomacy Delhi University**	Indian Foreign Services
4. **National Police Academy Hyderabad**	To train Indian Police Service
5. **Departmental Training School, Simla**	Training for Indian Audit and Accounts Service
6. **National Academy of Direct Taxes, Nagpur**	To train Income Tax officer
7. **National Academy of Customs, Excise and Narcotics, New Dehli.**	To train officers of excise and customs.
8. **Railway Staff College, Baroda**	To train Railway officers of traffic, transportation, Commercial Department, Railway Accounts Service

| 9. | Secretariat Training School, New Delhi | To train secretariat officers in organisation, office procedures, financial rules and regulations (upto Section Officers grade) |

32. INSTITUTES OF INDIA

S.No.	Conducting qualifying	Examination
1.	Indian Institute of Bankers	A.II.B.
2.	Institute of Chartered Accountants of India	C.A.
3.	Institute of Chartered Financial Analysts of India	C.F.A.
4.	Institute of Company Secretaries of India	A.C.S.
5.	Institute of Costs and Works Accountants of India	I.C.W.A
6.	Institute of Engineers	A.M.I.E
7.	Indian Institute of Finance	B.B.F., M.B.F.
8.	All India Management Association	P.G.D.M.
9.	Indian Statistical Institute	Dip. Stat.
10.	Computer Society of India	National Standard Examination

33. HIGHER EDUCATION (PROFESSIONAL)

S.No.	Council/Commission	to Recognise study
1.	University Grants Commission (U.G.C.) 1956 Estd.	Universities - 214 Deemed - 38 Colleges 9703
2.	All India Council of Technical Education (AICTE)	Engineering studies/ Institutions 372+ 876 Polytechnics

3.	**All India Medical Council**	Medical Institutions, Ayurvedic 120 Unani 27 Siddha Colleges 2
4.	**Dental Council of India**	Dental Institutions
5.	**The Pharmacy Council of India**	Pharmaceutical Institutions
6.	**Bar Council of India**	Legal Study Colleges
7.	**Indian Council of Agricultural Research**	Agricultural Colleges
8.	**All India Board of Management studies**	Management Studies
9.	**National Council of Management and Catering Technology**	Studies/Institutes of Hotel Management
10.	**Institute of Architects**	Study of Architecture
11.	**National Council of Teacher Education**	Study of Teacher Education

34. ACADEMIES IN INDIA

AWARDS

1.	**Sangeeth Natak Academy (1953)**	Development of Dance, Drama and Music
2.	**Lalith Kala Academy (1954)**	Understanding of Indian Arts, Painting, Sculpture and Graphic Art
3.	**Sahitya Academy (1954)**	Development of Indian Literature
4.	**Indian National Science Academy**	Outstanding contributions to research

35. NOBEL LAUREATES

1. **Rabindranath Tagore** (Literature) 1913
2. **Sir C.V. Raman** (Physics) 1930
3. **Mother Theresa** (Peace) 1979 (Yugoslavia born)
4. **Dr. Chandrasekhara Subramaniam** (India born) (Astrophysicist) - 1983
5. **Dr. Amarthya Sen** (Economics) 1998
6. **Hargobind Khorana** (India born) U.S. Scientist Nobel Prize (Medicine) 1968
7. **Dr. V.S. Naipaul** (India born)Trinidad (Literature) 2001

36. GOVT. OF INDIA AWARDS

Civilian Decorations

1. **BHARAT RATNA**

   India's highest civilian honour for distinguished and excellent service.

2. **PADMA VIBHUSHAN**

   Second highest civilian honour for distinguished service in any field including Govt. service.

3. **PADMA BHUSHAN**

4. **PADMA SRI**

CIVILIAN AWARDS

1. **PRESIDENT AWARD FOR BEST TEACHER.**

   National Teacher Award (and) Certificate of Honour. Silver Medal. Cash Rupees Ten thousand (By H.R.D. Ministry of Central Government.)

2. **BHATNAGAR AWARD**

   Outstanding scientist award by Council of Scientific and Industrial Research.

3. **DR. B. C. ROY AWARD**

   Outstanding medical experts (gold medal, citation, a trophy, cash award) Dr. B.C. Roy National Award Fund by Medical Council of India, since 1966.

CINEMA AWARDS

Ministry of Information and Broadcasting

1. **Dadha Saheb Phalke Award**

Awarded to veterans in cine field. Award comprises "Swarna Kamal", cash prize of Rupees One Lakh and a shawl.

2. **N.T.R. AWARD**

Awarded for outstanding contribution for the growth of Indian cinema.

Carries Rs 5 lakhs, citation and silver plate.

37. INTERNATIONAL AWARDS

1. **Magsaysay Awards (1957)**

To honour 5 Asians each year, who exemplify greatness of spirit, integrity and devotion to liberty.

Award carries gold medal, certificate, 10,000 U.S. dollars Five fields: 1. Govt. Service 2. Public Service 3. Community leadership 4. Journalism 5.International understanding.

2. **Kalinga Prize**

International Award presented each year by UNESCO. Awarded to person distinguished career of service in interpretation of science and research to public.

(UNESCO gold medal and invited to visit India)

3. **U Thant Award**

Awarded to outstanding persons, for enhancing cultural understanding and development between nations.

4. **Asan World Prize**

Award consists of a gold medal, a golden blosson and a scroll of honour.

38. INTERNATIONAL AWARDS
(Indian Awards)

1. **Gandhi Peace Prize - (1995)**

(Carries 10 million rupees, citation and plaque)

Awarded by Dept. of culture, G.O.I.

2. **Jawaharlal Nehru Award for International Understanding**

   Award carries 15 lakhs of rupees in cash, and citation. For contribution for international peace and understanding.

3. **Indira Gandhi Prize for Peace, Disarmament and Development.**

   (By Indira Gandhi Memorial Trust 1984) citation with 25 lakhs of rupees.

39. NATIONAL AWARDS

1. **Harmony Award**

   (For outstanding contribution to the promotion of Communal Harmony and National Integration)

   Citation, cash award one lakh (individuals) / 2 lakhs (for institutions) (By National Foundation for Communal Harmony under Home Ministry founded in 1995)

2. **Bharathiya Jnanpith Awards (1965)**

   Awarded to outstanding Indian Literature (carries 1 lakh)

3. **Rajiv Gandhi National Sadbhavana Award**

   Awarded for promoting good will and national harmony Cash prize of 2.5 lakhs.

4. **Jamnalal Bajaj Awards**

   Outstanding persons in various fields.

5. **Deshikothama Award**

   (Award instituted by Viswa Bharathi university)

6. **Rajiv Gandhi National Unity Award**

   Outstanding service in social political fields.

7. **Indira Gandhi National Integration Award**

40. SPORTS - AWARDS

H.R.D. Ministry Awards

1. **Rajiv Gandhi Khel Ratna Award (1991)**

   Carries citation, with three lakh cash for best sportsperson.

2. **Dronacharya Award**

   Carries citation and 2.5 lakh cash for Best coach.

3. **Maulana Abul Kalam Azad Trophy**

Carries citation with one lakh cash (for best all round performance)

4. **Arjuna Award**

Carries citation and cash award of one lakh rupees (for best player)

41. NATIONAL BRAVERY AWARDS-1957

For Children

Bravery Awards

(By Indian Council of Child Welfare)

1. Bharat Award

(Gold Medal and cash)

2. Geetha Chopra Award

(Silver Medal and Cash)

3. Sanjay Chopra Award

(Silver Medal and Cash)

4. Other Awards

(Silver Medal and Cash)

All awardees are given financial assistance for the schooling upto graduation.

42. BHARAT RATNA AWARDS

S.No	Year	Name	Remark
1.	1954	Dr. S. Radhakrishnan (1888-1975)	
2.	1954	C. Rajagopalachari (1879-1972)	
3.	1954	Dr. C. V. Raman (1888-1970)	(Nobel Laureate)
4.	1955	Dr. Bagawan Das (1869-1958)	
5.	1955	M. Visweswarayya (1861-1962)	
6.	1955	Jawaharlal Nehru (1889-1964)	
7.	1957	G.B. Pant (1887-1961)	
8.	1958	Dhondo Keshav Karve (1858-1962)	
9.	1961	Dr. B.C. Roy (1882-1962)	
10.	1961	P.D. Tandon (1882-1962)	

11.	1962	Dr. Rajendra Prasad (1884-1963)	
12.	1963	Dr. Zakir Hussain (1897-1969)	
13.	1963	Pandurang Vaman Kane (1880-1972)	
14.	1966	Lal Bahadur Sastry (1904-1966)	(Posthumous)
15.	1971	Indira Gandhi (1917-1984)	
16.	1975	V.V. Giri (1884-1980)	
17.	1976	K. Kamaraj (1903-1975)	Posthumous
18.	1980	Mother Teresa (1910-1997)	(Nobel Laureate)
19.	1983	Acharya Vinobha Bhave (1895-1982)	Posthumous
20.	1987	Khan Abdul Ghaffar Khan (1890-1988)	
21.	1988	M.G. Ramachandran (1917-1987)	Posthumous
22.	1990	B.R. Ambedkar (1891-1956)	Posthumous
23.	1990	Nelson Mandela (1918-)	
24.	1991	Morarji Desai (1896-1995)	
25.	1991	Rajiv Gandhi (1944-1991)	Posthumous
26.	1991	Vallabhai Patel (1875-1950)	Posthumous
27.	1992	J.R.D. Tata (1904-1993)	
28.	1992	Sathyajit Ray (1922-1992)	
29.	1992	Subash Chandra Bose (1897-1945)	Posthumous
30.	1992	Moulana Abul Kalam Azad (1888-1958)	Posthumous
31.	1997	Aruna Asaf Ali (1909-1996)	Posthumous
32.	1997	G.L. Nanda (1898-1997)	
33.	1997	A.P.J. Abdul Kalam (1931)	
34.	1998	M.S. Subbulakshmi (1916)	
35.	1998	C. Subramaniam (1910-2000)	
36.	1999	J.P. Narain (1902-1979)	Posthumous
37.	1999	Dr. Amarthya Sen (1933-)	
38.	1999	Pandit Ravi Shankar (1920-)	
39.	1999	Gopinath Bordoloi (1890-1950)	Posthumous
40.	1999	Jayaprakash Narayan (1902-1979)	Posthumous
41.	2000	Lata Mangeshkhar	
42.	2000	Ustad Bismillah Khan	

43. CENSUS OF INDIA

1.	First Census conducted in British rule	1871
2.	Conducted every	10 years
3.	Census Department made permanent Institution by an Act of Parliament in	1948
4.	9th Census and 1st Census of Independent India conducted in the year	1951
5.	Constitutional obligation	1) To determine territorial constituencies of Parliament and Assemblies
		2) To determine no. of seats to be allocated to S.C.s and S.T.s.

44. CENSUS 2001

1.	Conducted in no. of households	**200 millions**
2.	No. of villages	**6,40,100**
	No. of towns	**5161**
3.	Population	**102.7 crores**
	Males	**53.13 crores**
	Females	**49.57 crores**
4.	Literacy Rate	**65.38%**
	Males	**75.85%**
	Females	**54.16%**
5.	Population crossed 100 crores on	**11-05-2000**
6.	India's population to world population	**16.7%**
	Living in world's land area	**2.4%**

● ● ● ● ●